Zarqa Nawaz created *Little Mosque on the Prairie* for Canadian television, and has spent much of the past six years writing comedy pilots for ABC, CBS, NBC and FOX, and touring the world as a sought-after public speaker. She has been interviewed or profiled by CNN, the BBC, the *New York Times* and Al Jazeera. She lives in Regina with her family.

Laughing All the Way to the Mosque

ZARQA NAWAZ

virago

VIRAGO

First published in Canada in 2014 by HarperCollins Publishers Ltd
First published in Great Britain in 2015 by Virago Press

1 3 5 7 9 10 8 6 4 2

Copyright © 2014 by Zarqa Nawaz

The moral right of the author has been asserted.

A CIP catalogue record for this book
is available from the British Library.

ISBN 978-0-349-00593-5

Typeset in Bembo by M Rules
Printed and bound in Great Britain by
Clays Ltd, St Ives plc

Papers used by Virago are from well-managed forests
and other responsible sources.

MIX
Paper from
responsible sources
FSC® C104740

Virago Press
An imprint of
Little, Brown Book Group
100 Victoria Embankment
London EC4Y 0DY

An Hachette UK Company
www.hachette.co.uk

www.virago.co.uk

To my husband, Samiul Haque, who always consoles me with the words 'Sometimes grit is more important than talent.'

And to my parents, Parveen and Ali Nawaz, who instilled that grit at a very early age and made me believe it was talent.

Contents

Introduction

When I was seven, I went up to a little boy in the schoolyard. He was sitting alone on the swings, sucking on a jawbreaker. He had black wavy hair and was a little on the chubby side.

'Davy, do you believe in God?'

He shrugged.

'Because it's really, really important to believe in God.'

Davy, faced with a raging fundamentalist Muslim child, said:

'I'll believe in God if you push me on the swings for as long as I want.'

My arms ached and recess became torture, but I was happy to pay the price of saving Davy's soul.

A little while later, Davy's mother invited me to his birthday party. I was thrilled. I noticed that, as I sat at their table munching the snacks, she watched me with worry. 'Don't eat that,' she said.

'But it's yummy.' I stuffed more food into my face.

'That's ham,' she said, frowning. 'Aren't you Muslim?'

I stuffed the last pieces into my mouth as fast as my guilty conscience would allow. The meat was so good, it felt like eating a piece of heaven. I looked sadly at the tray of cold cuts that she quickly removed from my hypnotized gaze.

Davy's mother apologized to my mother when she came to pick me up.

'I just thought she would know what pork was.'

My mother looked at her greedy Muslim child and sighed.

'We send her to the mosque, but her attention span is limited.'

I was a little insulted. At least I had gotten the God part right. Who knew that the pictures of cute pigs with a giant X through them would translate to tasty morsels on a platter?

Davy looked at me with new interest.

'Are you going to hell now?'

'Of course not,' said his mother, appalled. 'She made a mistake, and like we learned in church, Davy, God forgives.'

'Davy goes to church?' I asked.

'Of course. We're Roman Catholic. Davy's a choirboy.'

After that day, I still pushed Davy on the swings, because it was the right thing to do, even if I had started for the wrong reasons. But I decided to pay more attention to my lessons at the mosque. God was probably teaching me a lesson: Worry about your own soul, which always seemed in constant peril. Religion was a tricky business.

When you grow up in the West, things sometimes get lost in translation. The other month I was responsible for organizing the mosque community potluck. My friend Faeeza and I watched guests arrive with dessert after dessert, and no main courses in sight.

'How did you arrange the potluck?' she asked.

'I asked the first half of the alphabet to bring dessert and the second half to bring a main dish.'

'You realize that the majority of Muslim last names fall into the first half of the alphabet, right? Ahmed, Abdullah, Ali . . . '

The dessert table overflowed with trays of baklava and boxes of doughnuts; we were forced to pile the sweets under the tables and in various corners of the room. Discontent was brewing. I could hear grumbling stomachs. I looked at the two sad little chicken dishes on the main-course table.

'Order pizza,' said Faeeza.

A few tardy Yusufs and Zakariahs brought a few more chicken dishes while we waited for the pizza. Even though we fast every year during Ramadan, my hungry Muslims could wait no longer. The crowd devoured the chicken and topped off with ample dessert and tea. By the time the twenty pizzas arrived, everyone was full and in the throes of a sugar-induced stupor. 'What are we going to do with all this pizza?' I asked Faeeza.

'Sell it?'

I took to the microphone.

'We are raising money for a new mosque. Everyone who buys a pizza will be contributing to the fund. They're ten dollars each.'

'By the way, how much were the pizzas?' I asked Faeeza after I came back from the podium.

'Twelve dollars.'

No one was volunteering to buy the pizzas. I went over to where the men were sitting. I figured they'd still be hungry.

'Ask my wife,' said Wael. 'She makes all the decisions in the family.'

Faheem, Abdul-Rahman and Gamal said the same thing. I gave up on the men and negotiated with the women. The women, of course, could smell our desperation and took pity on us and bought the pizzas.

A week later, my husband told me that a complaint had been emailed to the board of the Islamic Association.

'Oh no, someone's upset that there wasn't enough food?'

'No,' said Sami. 'One of the men reported that there was a woman who was fraternizing with the men too much: "The standard of the mosque potluck has fallen with all the lascivious gazing going on between the genders. How we can continue to call these events Islamic is beyond imagining."'

Rather than a culinary travesty, my potluck would go down in history as a sex scandal.

Recess

'Ummi, could you make me a sandwich, like the other kids?' I asked my mother as she wrapped curried chicken drumsticks in aluminium foil for my lunch.

My mother was the reason I was a social pariah. I would watch the other girls eat their neat little sandwiches while my lunch radiated smells like an onion-infused nuclear bomb. After lunch, all the kids at Fallingdale Elementary School went out for recess. The girls skipped rope while I sulked by the brick wall. My oily chicken legs were keeping me from assimilating. No one came near me because I was probably contagious. I wanted to be like Kathleen, with her long, shiny, blond hair, light, airy summer dresses and lunches that smelled like vanilla. Her hair, her clothes, her sandwich. I envied all three. Perhaps I could have one of them.

My poor mother sighed as she listened to my complaints.

'People look at me strangely when I eat those things,' I said, pointing. 'No one wants to play with me because of my lunch.' I was a clumsy carnivore among graceful herbivores.

The next day I walked to school armed with my sandwich – white bread, peanut butter and jelly – which smelled like candy instead of cumin. It was the aroma of triumph. I waited anxiously for lunchtime, and when it came I looked over at Kathleen, sinking her teeth into a chocolate doughnut. This was it. It was about to happen. I would open my brown-paper bag, pull out my waxed-paper-wrapped sandwich and suddenly my world would change. I'd be at Kathleen's house, and she'd let me comb her long blond hair while we talked about planning her ninth birthday party.

'What made you notice me?' I'd ask.

'The sandwich,' she'd say.

As I opened the aluminium-foil package – could my mother never be trained? – Kathleen turned and looked directly at my sandwich. It was working! Kathleen gave a little wave – to the cutest boy in our class, who was right behind me – before turning back to her shiny-haired friends. There wasn't enough white bread in the world to make me fit in with white kids.

As I sat dejected and hungry (it turns out that curry drumsticks are much more filling than peanut butter) on the carpeted floor with my grade-three classmates, I contemplated my options. The sandwich didn't work. The golden hair was out of the question. But maybe, just maybe, I could change my clothes.

I looked different from the other girls. It wasn't just because I was brown and had long braids. It was the way my mother dressed me. My clothes were odd. I looked over at Kathleen, who was wearing a miniskirt with a halter top. I was wearing brown cords with a matching corduroy shirt. She was the fairy princess and I was the ugly stepsister. But even ugly stepsisters could go shopping. If I could convince my mother to make me a sandwich, how hard could it be to convince her to let me wear a dress? I dragged my beleaguered mother to

Kmart and found a white peasant minidress that fell to my knees. It was perfect.

The next morning I ditched the corduroy, put on my beautiful white dress and looked at myself in the mirror. My legs were a little cold, never having been exposed to that much air before, but I looked like a brown princess. My mother had become my fairy godmother, and as I grabbed my sandwich on my way out the door, my metamorphosis was complete.

'You're not going out dressed like that,' my mother said, staring at my bare legs.

My mother was in traditional Pakistani clothes: the shalwar kameez, a long tunic with baggy trousers. To her, wearing a dress without trousers meant you were half naked, like forgetting to put on your shirt, going to school topless.

I dutifully returned upstairs and put on my cords under my dress. I looked in the mirror again. My fairy godmother was actually a fairy godmonster and had reversed the spell.

When I was five, hanging on to the ears of a giant red rubber ball, happily bouncing down the street in Liverpool, my father had called me over. 'We are moving to Canada,' he said.

Now I was eight. I wanted to tell my parents that I didn't fit in, but I realized *they* didn't fit in either. They had left behind their entire lives to make a better one for their children. Being in Canada meant opportunities that a life in rural Pakistan or even in Liverpool couldn't provide, and for that they were grateful. But I, their only daughter, who'd had no say and had been forced to leave behind, among other things, a giant red bouncy ball, was not grateful at all. I was ugly, and to me that was worse than being a starving child with maimed limbs in Karachi, Pakistan. In Brampton, Ontario, I was the only brown girl in my class.

When I came home for lunch, corduroy pants brushing noisily under my dress, I must have looked extra-sullen.

'Why are you here?' my mother asked. I pulled out the sandwich that had failed to fix everything that was wrong with my life and munched on it sadly. 'I'd rather just eat at home.'

'What's wrong?'

'The kids don't like me. I have no friends.'

'Did someone tell you that?'

'No one says anything to me, Ummi,' I said. 'It's like I'm invisible.'

'You should try harder,' she said.

I did, I thought to myself. But someone made me wear trousers under my dress.

I knew that my mother's childhood in Pakistan had been a happy time. Her family's wealth meant she always dressed in the most fashionable clothes and was one of the most popular girls in her class. If anyone had had the power to be a bully, it was my mother. My father used to tell me that she had servants to wash and iron her clothes and get her ready in the morning. My mother would vehemently deny these stories as horrible exaggerations, but I noticed that every wool sweater of mine that she washed wound up a shrunken scrap of felt.

My mother regarded me, her ugly duckling.

'I'm coming to school with you.'

I looked up to where I thought God must live, thinking, Am I not suffering enough?

Surely if God could create an entire universe in seven epochs, erect mountains and fill oceans full of resplendent creatures, he could find a way to let me wear a dress without trousers. But no, in his limitless glory, God's solution was to have my mother come to school with me. She was the mothership of uncoolness,

and I had unwittingly unleashed her. I assumed I was being punished for complaining.

The playground was full of children, mostly girls with
spaghetti-strap tops and short skirts that revealed snatches of
brightly patterned underwear when they jumped rope. I could
see the shock on my mother's face. This was not going to help
me shed the trousers from under my dress. She stopped in the
middle of the playground, surveying the lie of the land with
the authority of a general assessing the battlefield. She spotted
the leader, Kathleen, *my Kathleen*, who was wielding the skipping rope.

'Excuse me,' said my mother. 'Can my daughter play with
you?'

Kathleen looked first at my mother and then at me. She
was obviously confused by the sight of a sad, petulant child
wearing a summer dress with brown corduroy trousers in the
radiating heat, sporting braids that had gone out of style a
hundred years ago, standing beside a large Pakistani woman
in a long shirt and baggy pantaloons ballooning like sails
in the wind. My mother looked like a pirate and I her
oppressed first-mate. I mouthed a silent prayer: God, please
kill me now.

'Sure, she can play,' said Kathleen, and handed me the rope
so I could take over. My mother went home. I learned that
until a girl tripped, the rope turners weren't allowed back into
the game, and today nobody was falling down. By a bizarre
turn of events, Kathleen too had been freed from bondage.

It turns out that skipping rope in the playground was a mer-
itocracy: so as long as my wrists still worked I was allowed into
their circle, even if I was dressed for the wrong century.
Apparently all I had to do was ask. God clearly works in mysterious ways.

The next week, as my mother packed my sandwich, I looked at her.

'What's wrong?' she asked. 'Do you want tuna instead of peanut butter?'

'Could you put the chicken drumsticks back into my lunch?' I asked. 'I kinda miss them.'

Hairy Legs

My eight-year-old brother Muzammal took our baby brother, who we called Dutch even though his real name was Muddaththir – both of them named because our parents couldn't think of longer or more unpronounceable names – into the bathroom and locked the door. He took out my father's razor and drew it over Dutch's face. The blade immediately cut his cheek, and there was blood and screaming everywhere.

'What are you doing?' shrieked my poor mother when she finally got the bathroom door open.

'Shaving Dutch,' said Muzammal, as if it were the most logical thing in the world.

I hid because I didn't want the blame to fall where it should have – on my freshly shaved legs.

Shaving my legs had required the stealth and persistence of a trained spy. In our house, my father's face was the only thing that was shaved.

It was all because of gym class. Gym class didn't exist for my mother, growing up in Islamabad. She and her friends skipped rope during their breaks for exercise, legs and arms safely covered by their cotton shalwar kameez. My mother had never seen anyone in shorts until she came to Canada. Good Muslims don't wear shorts, was her belief. But if it was a requirement for this mysterious gym class, she'd relent. The shorts weren't an issue for me. It was what they revealed: hairy legs! God had made my mother hairless, so it was easy for her to take the moral high ground, which was that shaving legs was un-Islamic. Only white people did things like that.

'The kids in gym class stare at me.'

'Ignore them.'

But they wouldn't ignore me and I couldn't blame them either, because the ugly truth was that, when it came to hair, I was my father's daughter.

Once, as a young man living in England, my father went swimming in the local pool. As he waded in, the thick, curly black hair that covered his entire body expanded and rose in the water, and the children in the pool screamed and ran out. They thought a bear had just fallen into the pool.

I inherited that hairy gene, and I didn't need a swimming pool to be mistaken for something that belonged in a zoo. The hair on my legs was long, thick and black. I complained bitterly to my mother – it was her fault that this hairy gene afflicted me.

'You had an arranged marriage. Why didn't you ask the matchmaker to pull up Daddy's trouser leg?'

'Your father had a good job,' replied my mother.

My Sikh friend Jasminder and I compared our legs and commiserated with each other. Neither of our mothers was a leg-shaver.

'Someone told me once that tarantulas are the Marilyn Monroes of the insect world,' said Jas.

'No one's mistaking me for a blond beauty,' I replied sadly.

I made up every excuse to get out of gym class. I had the flu, I had cramps, I had cramps with the flu. The poor gym teachers had no idea what was wrong with me but it seemed to be contagious: Jas had it too.

Desperate, Jas and I scoured our school rules for an exception to the uniform. And there, like a mirage in the desert, floated the word that would save us: 'leotards'. Jas and I locked eyes; our torment was over. I marched straight home after school and convinced my father to buy me black tights and a one-piece bodysuit to wear on top.

The wait for gym class was agony, but the time finally arrived after lunch. While the other girls changed out in the open, I hid with my furry legs in a toilet cubicle. After all the other girls, including Jas, had filed out into the gym, I emerged from my creaky stall like a butterfly from her cocoon. Examining myself in the mirror, I was a triumph. Not a hair in sight. I tied up my laces and trotted out to the gym floor, ready to be newly embraced by my classmates.

The entire class came to a standstill. I was tall and gangly for my age: I was a giant black spider in white gym shoes.

I heard a snicker. Someone whistled. In a panic, my eyes desperately searched for Jas, who was surely also revamped into a spider. When I found her, she was looking just as astonished at me as the others. Her oversized T-shirt fell gently over her black leggings. I was a fool. A Spandex-wrapped fool.

This was it. I snuck into my parents' bathroom to find my father's razor. He had the old-fashioned kind, where you had to unscrew the metal top, insert a double-edged blade and reassemble. I locked the door. I didn't know anything about using a razor or the usefulness of shaving cream. So I hacked at my dry legs as if through a forest with a butter knife. It was time-consuming and painful, but it worked. For the first time in my life, I had finally rid myself of the dreaded hair.

My father must have wondered why his razor was always dull, but neither he nor my mother was any the wiser. With two boys under nine, my parents weren't paying attention to me – but Muzammal was. Muzammal was one year younger then me. Watching my comings and goings with my father's razor made him curious about shaving, and what better way to find out how razors work than to shave our one-year-old baby brother?

After Dutch was stitched up at the emergency room my father decided to hide the razor blades. Something strange was going on with their kids, and they couldn't figure out what.

All the hair grew back on my legs.

One day during my Qur'an study class at the mosque, I asked my teacher, Sister Maryam, the question that was tormenting me. After all, I didn't want to burn in hell because I shaved my legs, a sin that seemed to be up there with murder and eating bacon, but then again, gym class was hell on earth.

'Is it un-Islamic to shave your legs?' I asked.

'Let me see your legs,' she asked. I pulled up my trousers.

'For you, it might be un-Islamic if you *didn't* do something about that.'

I told her my sad razor-blade story. She was appalled I had even thought about becoming a leg-shaver.

'It makes the hair grow back thicker,' she said.

I was horrified. That was *possible*?

'You have to rip the hair out from the root, and eventually it will never come back.'

Ripping hair out from the root sounded painful. But anything would be less painful than the stares in gym class.

Sister Maryam taught me how to make *halawa*. It took a lot

of practice and patience. I almost gave up, but life was too short and my hair was too long.

I would boil water, sugar and lemon juice until it turned into a sticky golden goo. I would roll it into a ball, apply it to my legs, then after a few minutes rip the halawa off. It was like applying napalm to your legs. It burned. Not deterred, I boiled halawa like my life depended on it.

My mother watched incredulously but couldn't complain. In her mind, Arabs trumped South Asians when it came to Islam, since Arabs speak Arabic, the language of the Qur'an. And since Arabs, like Sister Maryam, are manic about hair removal, hair removal couldn't be un-Islamic. Going to the mosque had finally paid off. I joined the track team. My teammates overlooked my strange, patchy appearance – I looked like a leopard, with random tufts of hair that I'd missed – and we broke the school record in the hundred-metre relay.

My mother must have wondered at how Islam seemed to evolve when you leave your home country. Hair removal had gone from sin to religious requirement.

Hijab

Throwing away the conventions with which our parents raised us helps us define who we are. Short hair was part of my plan to burn and pillage my parents' world view.

Aunty Firoza appraised the black waves that fell down past my waist all the way to my butt.

'Cut it all off,' I said.

'That's pretty dramatic.'

'Exactly.'

'How do your parents feel about this?' asked Aunty Firoza as she slowly worked the blades of my mother's giant sewing scissors through my hair.

'They're fine,' I said. It was technically true. My mother had resigned herself to my decision but refused to wield the scissors, so I'd had to ask her friend. My father was definitely opposed. Whenever I mentioned it, he'd pull out the Qur'an and say it was forbidden. All he could point to, though, was a verse about following the Prophet. My father said that the Prophet Muhammad would not approve, and therefore he didn't either. In my father's world, a woman's hair was her glory. In mine, it was a pain in the ass.

'Why can't I cut my hair?' I had asked my mother.

'Only modern Muslims do things like that,' she said.

'Modern' Muslims acted like white people. They had short hair, wore miniskirts and, the biggest heresy of all, talked to boys on the phone.

There is no Islamic prohibition about cutting hair. I was just facing the last remnant of my parents' old-world mentality. I decided my parents must be terrible Muslims – what other explanation was there for people who invoked non-existent verses of the Qur'an to prop up arbitrary rules? I'd had enough. The hair had to go: partly because I was done with looking like I belonged on *Little House on the Prairie*, but mostly because it would drive my parents crazy.

When Aunty Firoza finished with the scissors, I was left with a bad but serviceable bob. The last time my hair had been this short, I was five. I felt totally liberated. I had won another battle against my parents' restrictive lifestyle. My father was livid, but he couldn't yell at another man's wife. Plus he didn't have a religious leg to stand on. Aunty Firoza avoided his gaze and quickly went home. My mother consoled him: they had come to a new land, things had to change.

But to make sure they didn't change too much, my parents sent Muzammal and me to Muslim camp every summer, and this summer was no different, except I went triumphant with my new hair.

Triumphant because in actual fact this camp was full of city-slicker, modern Muslims with short haircuts and tight jeans. It was just like white-people camp except everyone was brown. My brother and I were the equivalent of backward, illiterate village Muslims in comparison. My parents clearly didn't know what was going on, and the two of us were thrilled and kept our mouths shut. To us Muslim summer camp was an escape from our parents, and I suppose they probably felt the same way about it.

When I went to camp that summer, I noticed a new person on staff: an Egyptian woman hired to be the camp doctor. She was beautiful and luminous. But she was different: her hair was neatly covered with a headscarf, a hijab.

I had never before heard of a hijab. Whenever my father drove my brother and me to the mosque, I covered my hair with a flimsy piece of cloth that sat halfway off my head. I would whip it off as soon we drove away and never thought enough about it to consider it could have a name. My aunts in Pakistan wore the burqa, and my mother wore a dupatta, which is a chiffon-like cloth that she would wear loosely over her head, Benazir Bhutto-style, during prayers. The point was just to cover your head: even modern Muslim women placed paper napkins on their head when they heard Arabic spoken at a community potluck.

But the hijab was a new way of being modest. And it came with very strict rules: no hair, no neck and no ears could show. Even my supposedly conservative Muslim mother didn't cover her hair like that. Clearly, I had not been guided correctly in our faith.

The doctor complained to the camp organizers that we weren't being taught the correct way of dressing in Islam. 'Why are all the girls wearing T-shirts and jeans?'

For me, dressing as a Muslim girl meant wearing long, baggy tops and pants. I wasn't following any specific rules, just looking unfashionably bad. This hijab-wearing doctor was a revelation. The hijab was not like the dupatta, sliding on and off according to the whims of the weather or the wearer. The hijab was like a uniform, attached to your head with pins and ties. Gale-force winds could not tear the hijab off a devout woman's head. Was this a way to be *even more* Muslim than my parents? Intriguing . . .

After camp that summer, there was a buzz about hijabs in our mosque. A friend of mine, Aliya, decided to wear one full-time. This meant she would wear it to school, and even to the mall – where everyone would be able to see her. Two weeks later, Sameena decided to wear the hijab full-time as well. It was like a virus, spreading among the girls. Every week another friend took up the hijab. After all, it made sense of the lectures that we attended at the mosque, about the tyranny of the beauty industry and how Islam freed us by giving us back our dignity.

'A woman's body should be protected from the indecent gaze of a man.'

A man's indecent gaze had never lingered upon me, but I liked the theory.

'You wouldn't take a diamond necklace through Harlem unprotected, and a woman is more precious than a diamond, so why should she go uncovered?'

Somehow the racist, sexist perfection of this statement rang true in my unsuspicious, malleable young mind. I was more precious than a diamond! There was even a verse in the Bible that said women should cover their hair. Every picture of Mary, the mother of Jesus, showed her hair covered. Nuns covered too.

But the best thing about hijab was that I had discovered it on my own – my parents had nothing to do with it. I could beat them at their own game: religion. Some people think the hijab is used to oppress women. I used it to oppress my parents.

'I'm wearing a hijab to school,' I told them as I wrapped a

sky-blue piece of georgette around my head, proud of my über-religious state.

They were stunned at first, but then my father decided wearing hijab would mean I'd have more time to devote to school and not boys, which was fine by him. I was disappointed by his lack of outrage (and impressed with his fantasy about me and boys), but my mother reacted in a way I could never have predicted. She stared gape-mouthed at my clumsily wrapped blue head. How could she be dressed less modestly than her daughter? She had no choice but to wear hijab as well. I was furious – the hijab was *my* thing. How dare my mother adopt it as her own? But my anger quickly turned into that other primary teenage emotion: humiliation. My mother had always worn an elegant shalwar kameez with a diaphanous dupatta. She looked different from the other mothers at school, but beautiful in her own way. Unfortunately, she had no idea how to wear a hijab. Her severe cotton headscarf made her head resemble a tuna can. I was embarrassed to be seen with her in the mall.

'Just take it off,' I yelled when we went out together.

She couldn't. She felt that if wearing hijab was part of her religion, then she had to do it.

Since my parents had ruined my hijab rebellion, I refused to let my religious fervor stop at my head. I started treating my hijab like a magic wand. I could wave my holier-than-thou hijab-covered head and complain about whatever I wanted. This wasn't a privilege I'd been afforded when I was just a bare-headed Muslim.

'Wow, you guys get interest on your bank account?' I asked my mother. I informed the gobsmacked bank teller that, unlike my neglectful parents, I would not be engaging in usury.

'Plucking eyebrows is forbidden,' I told my mother's friends.

'There's alcohol in vanilla extract, and you've used it for how many years?' I said as I threw my mother's bottle into the garbage.

'How dare you listen to music?' I said and turned off my father's Bollywood tunes.

'You guys are like modern Muslims who don't even know about their own religion!'

I scoured the *hadith* for details of seventh-century Muslim life. When my bed broke I wouldn't let my parents buy me a new one. I slept in a sleeping bag on my carpeted floor. Authentic Muslims didn't use box springs, I said.

'Beds are not forbidden in Islam,' said my father, uneasy at my nit-picking approach to faith.

'I think you'll find God would approve,' I said.

When my mother took me to have my shalwar kameez sewn for Eid, I argued non-stop.

'I want long, loose shirts,' I told the seamstress as she measured my waist.

'I'm going to take it in at the waist to give it some shape,' she said innocently.

'No shape,' I said.

'But it won't look good,' she said. 'You'll look like you're wearing a sack.'

'That's exactly what I want.'

The seamstress implored my mother with her eyes to intervene, but my mother knew better. There was nothing she could do. I looked like I was wearing a giant paper bag for Eid. I loved it.

Bringing their children to the West was supposed to be about improving their quality of life. Instead, my parents were being told by their daughter that they weren't good Muslims.

And their daughter seemed to be throwing away the conveniences of modernity – such as beds. They just listened patiently to my droning. And then their patience paid off.

In late May, Uncle Mahmood, one of my father's oldest friends, convened a meeting of our two families. His daughter Zereena had gone to camp with me last year. We both had a blast. I was looking forward to talking to Zereena about our plans for camp that summer. I had an enormous suitcase, which I could barely close. Were ten outfits too many?

As we gathered in his living room, though, Uncle Mahmood was clearly upset. My expansive teenage imagination assumed the worst: he'd make us weigh our suitcases and enforce a ten-kilo limit. But it was much worse than that.

'At this so-called Muslim camp, they let the kids eat Chicken McNuggets. The children should be forbidden from attending this camp again,' he intoned.

Halal meat is a big issue for South Asian Muslims like us, so our family bought meat only from halal butchers. But Arab Muslims believed that meat slaughtered by Christians and Jews was acceptable and went on blind faith that someone of that religion was slaughtering the meat they bought at the local grocery store; no one was going to quiz the butchers on how often they went to church or synagogue.

I couldn't believe my ears. I loved Muslim camp more than life itself. 'You're not being fair,' I said out loud before I had a chance to think. 'It's a good camp and I really like going.'

My father watched the exchange with interest.

'There's a difference of opinion about meat,' I said, racking my brain for the religious niceties and coming up empty.

'There's only one real opinion, and proper Muslims follow that one,' said Uncle Mahmood.

I had turned my faith into endless rules. They had given me

structure. They had helped me torture my parents. And now they were being thrown back at me.

My father had heard enough. He looked steadily at me as he said, 'My daughter is right. We have to be more flexible when it comes to faith. We can't be extremists when it comes to Islam, can we?'

And in one fell swoop, my father dismissed the meeting and said I could go to summer camp as long as I wanted. In that moment, I decided not to take Islam so literally. Maybe God had sent me a sign through those Chicken McNuggets. Even though I had a strange haircut and paraded around in my hijab as if I was the Pope, my father stuck up for me because I was his little girl and he knew what summer camp meant to me. My parents were good Muslims and it wouldn't kill me to become a little more like them.

'I'm thinking about growing out my hair,' I said.

'It's fine short,' my father said. 'But how about you sleep in a bed?'

I agreed.

Muslim Summer Camp

I needed a sign from God. My future was in peril.

My first year at university was off to an abysmal start. I'd been a star in high school, where everything had been easy. But at university, nothing was easy. Calculus and chemistry were bad, but physics was unfathomable. Newton and his three laws were killing me. I was in freefall.

Partly in desperation, partly out of procrastination, I decided to escape the library for Friday prayers. I was happily being sucked into the mosque's gravitational field. I'm sure Newton would have approved. I packed up my twenty kilos of textbooks and drove to Jami Mosque, a Presbyterian church built in downtown Toronto in 1910 that had been converted into a mosque in the 1960s. In Muslim countries, mosques are decorated with colourful, hand-crafted tiles organized in intricate geometric patterns based on mathematical principles, in order to create complex designs that represent the unity of God's creation. These incredible works of art sometimes took decades to create. The exterior of Jami Mosque was also decorated with tiles – gleaming white bathroom tiles, to be precise. The well-meaning Muslims in charge of this mosque seemed to have the same understanding of mathematical concepts as I did. The neat straight rows of tile outlined the entire structure, with some Arabic calligraphy painted on. It reminded me of an eccentric Middle Eastern gingerbread house. Normally this would make me laugh but today I didn't care. I was going to the gingerbread mosque hoping God would send me some sort of a sign. After all, a mosque is a place where God is worshipped, *ergo* the place where God's signs should appear. I'm sure that was Newton's first law.

I solemnly climbed the stairs to the women's section in the old choir balcony, and sat with the other women. I had come all this way for a message from God. Instead I heard a sermon about the importance of being nice to one's neighbours. I felt a little deflated. I was mired in indecision about what to do next with my life, and an admonition to send a muffin basket next door didn't give me the guidance I was looking for.

Then came the community announcements.

'We are looking for volunteers to organize Muslim summer camp,' said Abdullah, a burly man who sounded a bit like Bob Marley, with a rich, deep voice that soothed my addled brain.

Clearly, this was the sign I was looking for.

'Where are you going?' asked my mother as I put on a headscarf to go out.

'To the mosque,' I said. 'I'm organizing Muslim summer camp.'

'Shouldn't you be studying for your exams? You need high grades to get into medical school.'

'They don't just look at your grades,' I said. 'They look at your volunteer work too. It might be even more important than grades.'

My mother looked at me sceptically.

'This is what God wants me to do,' I said, appealing to her religious side.

'Did you hear God say that to you?' she asked, knitting her eyebrows and looking more than a little concerned.

'No, of course not,' I replied, more than a little offended.

'Because if you're hearing voices, we can get you help.'

'I'm not hearing voices,' I said, now totally offended. 'I *sense* that God would want me to organize Muslim summer camp.'

'I *sense* you may be doing this to avoid studying.'

'Please.' I wound my winter scarf around my neck. 'I am not that shallow when it comes to God.'

The meeting was in one of the mosque's warren of rooms. I sat in an old-fashioned child-size metal desk which doubled as a storage cubby. It was full of broken crayons and a workbook with childish Arabic script. This was the same place I had learned how to read the Qur'an during Islamic weekend school. It brought back unpleasant memories of memorizing prayers in Arabic: I prefer to talk to God in English, so that nothing is lost in translation. There were several seventeen-year-olds who had volunteered to be camp counsellors. At twenty, I was the oldest. Abdullah was at the blackboard, writing out the different things that needed to be organized: registration, transportation, food, programming and recreational activities.

I approached him. 'I'd like to volunteer for the programming and recreational activities.'

'That's a lot to organize,' said Abdullah. 'Aren't you a university student?'

'I feel that's what God wants me to do,' I replied.

'You're not hearing voices, are you?' asked Abdullah, looking worried. 'It's just that young people your age tend to get overenthusiastic about religion.'

'I'm not a zealot,' I replied. Volunteering shouldn't be this hard, I thought. 'I'm just doing my Islamic duty.'

'What are you studying?'

'Science,' I replied. 'I'm trying to get into medical school.'

'Ah,' said Abdullah. 'Now it makes sense. You're having trouble with physics, aren't you? The creatively unfulfilled types always wind up on the programming committee.'

'Physics is very creative,' I managed. 'All those equations about giant balls that float.'

'You mean planets?' he said.

I changed the subject back to the camp.

'I've got really great ideas for the programme.'

Abdullah scratched his beard. 'Let's hear them.'

I racked my brain for all the Islamic lessons I had listened to while sitting at my metal desk as a child. Mostly they were about how to avoid hellfire and brimstone. Don't back-bite, be good to your mother, give money to poor people, don't lie – especially to your mother. (These all made the six-year-old me feel guilty.) And no premarital relations until after you're married. (We used to wonder what a premarital relation was – a third cousin?) It was standard stuff for weekend mosque classes.

'We could talk to the kids about how to become better Muslims,' I said. 'No back-biting, no lying—'

'Or we could put up wallpaper with scenes of the wilderness down here and save ourselves the trip,' said Abdullah. 'I want you to think outside the box.'

I liked my Muslim box. Its fire-and-brimstone fixation was comfortable.

'Well, my brother runs the Red Cross leadership camps,' I said. 'I could ask him for ideas.'

'Do that,' said Abdullah. Muzammal had been running the Red Cross international development education conferences for several years. They had simulation exercises: people pretending to be other people, debates about controversial subjects. It was pretty exciting stuff. Maybe too exciting for Muslims. I wrote out my ideas and took them to the mosque the next weekend.

'Now this is thinking outside the box,' said Abdullah.

I was relieved. I worked on my programme for the next few weeks while studying took a back seat.

'I'm going on a trip to Pakistan in July,' my mother said. 'Would you like to come?'

'It's the same time as Muslim camp,' I said. 'You know I can't make it. My responsibilities are too great.'

'It's just camp,' said my mother. 'You can leave if you want to.'

'My role is *crucial*,' I lied, knowing that Abdullah was really in charge. But for the first time since high school I was enjoying myself. It fed a part of my self-confidence that had been eroded by university. I was finally good at something again.

The night before camp was to start, I got an emergency call from Abdullah.

'Zarqa, I've broken my foot,' he said.

'What do you mean?'

'What I mean is that you're in charge of the Muslim camp programme.'

'But I don't know what I'm doing,' I said. 'You were supposed to supervise me.'

'You'll have to do it,' he said. 'We have thirty campers

registered. The counsellors will look after the kids. You just have to run the programme.'

I wondered if this was my punishment from God. Islamic weekend school was right: Don't lie to your mother.

I slept fitfully that night and woke exhausted. Abdullah wasn't coming. I was in charge. This was worse than physics. In the morning, I went to the mosque and boarded the bus with thirty kids under the age of fifteen.

'Where's Brother Abdullah?' asked Ibrahim, the head male counsellor.

'He's not coming,' I said, noting the look of panic in his eyes.

'But who's going to be in charge?' asked Lumya, the head female counsellor.

'Me,' I said, with as much authority as I could muster.

Lumya and Ibrahim looked at each other. I could read their minds: How could God do this to them? Welcome to the club, I thought.

'Well, it's a seven-hour bus ride to the camp grounds. We'll just sing songs until we get there,' I said.

'Let's pray to God for protection instead,' said Ibrahim solemnly.

Once we got to the site, everyone unpacked and chose cabins. As we ate dinner, I planned the next morning's events. I went to find Dwayne, the camp cook, to ask if he had any cardboard boxes. Dwayne was in his early thirties and had clearly never met any Muslims before. We were like a group of Martians who had just landed on his planet, and he was very excited.

'Why do you need boxes?' asked Dwayne. 'Is it a Muslim thing? Do you use them in your worship rituals?'

'No, I need them for a camping exercise tomorrow,' I said.

Dwayne looked disappointed but found me a pile of boxes.

After breakfast the next morning, Ibrahim and Lumya came to find me.

'So what's happening?' asked Ibrahim nervously. 'Are we going to have Islamic lectures like the last camp I went to?'

'You heard Brother Abdullah,' I said. 'He didn't want a regular Muslim camp, he wanted an exciting one.'

'Muslims don't do excitement,' said Ibrahim.

'Muslims do lectures about how to be better Muslims,' said Lumya, nodding knowingly.

'Yeah, well, this camp is different,' I said, wondering why it had to be. I gathered the campers outside and mixed up the groups so each contained girls and boys.

'Why are you doing that?' asked Ibrahim nervously.

'They're supposed to be a family,' I said. 'Families have both genders.'

'But intermingling between the sexes could be dangerous,' said Ibrahim. 'Something inappropriate could happen.'

'Like sex?' I said, irritated. 'Trust me, it's not that easy.' I had figured out what premarital relations were by now. No one was going to make it to first base in a cardboard box under my watch.

I gave each group a pile of boxes and explained the game. 'In many developing countries, people have very little to build their houses with,' I said, as if I knew what I was talking about. I myself had grown up in the suburbs of Toronto and only knew about aluminium siding. 'So your task today is to build your family a home using only the materials you have in front of you.'

The kids were excited. And after about twenty minutes I was gazing at six makeshift homes.

'Now what?' said Ibrahim, unimpressed. 'The kids have

learned they can make boxes out of cardboard boxes.'

Ibrahim was starting to irritate me.

'OK. kids, now I want every group to sit inside their houses,' I said. 'When the weather gets rough, we have our houses to protect us. Let's find out if your house can withstand a rainstorm.'

'How are you going to do that?' asked Lumya.

'I'm going to throw a bucket of water on each house,' I replied.

'Can I throw the water on the houses?' asked Ibrahim, thawing a little.

'Knock yourself out,' I said.

Ibrahim took a bucket and doused each house in turn. Only one of the six didn't collapse.

'This was almost fun,' said Ibrahim.

A twelve-year-old girl named Maria came up to us. She was crying.

'My grandmother lives in Pakistan,' she said. 'Is it a developing country?'

'Some parts of it,' I said.

'Is my grandmother's house going to fall down when it rains?'

I wondered if the Red Cross organizers ever had this problem.

'No,' I said. 'My grandmother is from Pakistan, too, but she lives in a house made with . . . aluminium siding.' What *was* my grandmother's house made of? I probably should have gone for that visit with my mother.

'I want to phone my nani and make sure she's OK.'

'The phones at the camp only call as far as Toronto. But how about we go swimming instead, and we'll call your parents tomorrow?'

That seemed to mollify her.

That evening, the kids all gathered in the community hall for the sunset and night prayers. Since we were travelling, we had special dispensation to combine the two prayers. We laid out the broken cardboard boxes, which had dried in the sun.

'So cardboard *is* a vital part of your religion,' said Dwayne.

'No,' I said patiently. 'It just protects our knees when we pray.' He was disappointed. I felt guilty, like we should be weirder just to make him happy.

'What are you gonna pray for?' he asked.

'Not to be in charge of this camp,' I said. 'And to be able to sprout my second head, finally.'

'Would you have to cover both your heads with a scarf?' he asked, looking at me hopefully.

Ibrahim wanted to know what we had in store for the night programme.

'It's going to be a lecture, right?' he asked hopefully.

'No,' I replied. 'It's going to be a debate about the merits of state schools versus full-time Islamic schools.'

'I attended a full-time Islamic school,' said Ibrahim. 'And I know it's better.'

'Well, I attended a full-time state school, and I think it's better.'

'It's obvious that you don't have a proper grasp of Islam,' said Ibrahim. 'If you went to Islamic school, we would have proper etiquette between the boys and girls.'

'Excuse me,' said Lumya. 'Has the debate started?'

Again I put the kids into mixed-gender teams and let each team debate the issue. Ibrahim was clearly uncomfortable with this sort of arrangement.

'I doubt they'll have sex while debating,' I assured him.

'Please don't make fun of me,' he steamed.

I was being hard on him. If something did happen, the parents would be furious. With me. The kids, however, loved it.

'We never get to argue about stuff like this in the mosque,' said Musa, a fifteen-year-old boy. 'When I get home I'm gonna tell my parents all the reasons why they should pull me out of Islamic school.'

I decided to move on to the nightly recreation. Traditionally, Muslims performed skits, which were excruciatingly boring: for example, a girl dressed up as the Qur'an, crying because everyone wants to watch TV and no one wants to read her. I wanted to come up with something that no one had ever done at Muslim camp before. There was a popular show on television called *The Newlywed Game*, where couples competed to answer tricky questions about their new spouses. In retrospect, I maybe should have stayed inside that box ...

'But no one here is married.' Ibrahim looked confused.

'But that's what makes it so fun,' I replied.

'We can't put the girls and boys together for a game like this.'

'Even I know that,' I said, insulted that my Islamic credentials were being questioned. 'The boys will be paired with boys, and the girls will be paired with girls.'

'You mean a boy has to pretend to be a wife?'

'Well, he can't have a female wife,' I replied. 'Or we risk premarital relations.'

'Fine,' said Ibrahim. 'Give me the questions.'

Ibrahim took his groups to another part of the mess hall. The first question was easy.

Question 1: What chocolate bar best describes your husband's intelligence?

Possible answers: Cadbury's Thick Chocolate Bar; Cadbury's Flake; Aero.

'I get it,' said Lumya. 'The chocolate bars are metaphors for our husband's intelligence.'

'Yeah,' I said.

Question 2: What movie reminds you of your husband when he kisses you?

Possible answers: *Jaws*; *Sudden Impact*; *Splash*.

'I get it,' said Lumya. 'The movies are a euphemism for your husband's technique for kissing.' She was swift.

Question 3: What British rock band best describes your husband on your wedding night?

Because the game was about married people, I had thought sex wouldn't be such a big deal ... I was wrong. Possible answers: Orchestral Manoeuvres in the Dark; Half Man, Half Biscuit; Throbbing Gristle.

Lumya came up to me. She was quivering slightly.

'This question refers to sex, right?' she whispered.

Ibrahim came up to me.

'I'm not that uptight,' he said, surprising me. 'It's just, for guys this is ... '

'Uncomfortable,' I supplied. 'OK, I get it. Let's make S'mores by the campfire and tell jinn stories!'

The kids were excited. Dwayne brought out marshmallows, crackers and chocolate.

'Is it OK if I join you?' he asked. 'I love campfires.'

'Sure,' I said.

'Is this part of your religion?'

'It's kind of a ritual at Muslim camp,' I replied, taking the marshmallows from him. 'Kind of like ghost stories at white-people camp.'

As the kids chanted 'S'mores! S'mores! S'mores!' around me, it dawned on me: this bag wasn't from the halal butcher store. Marshmallows can be a very controversial subject among

Muslims because they contain gelatin, and sometimes gelatin is sourced from pigs' feet. Halal marshmallows have gelatin made from plants.

I pulled Ibrahim to one side.

'We can't use these,' I hissed at him.

'You can't make a S'more without marshmallows,' said Ibrahim, much too loudly.

'Shhh! Keep your voice down! These marshmallows are a little fishy,' I said. 'We don't know the source of the gelatin. It could be from a pig!' I could feel my pulse racing.

Ibrahim looked surprisingly unprovoked. 'Look, God says don't eat pork. This is a marshmallow, not a chop. The gelatin in it is so highly processed, you can't even really consider it pork-related any more.'

I was speechless. This guy had been Mr Muslim all day, but he was OK with dubious marshmallows?

'But aren't we hiding something serious from the kids?' I said, feeling as if I had just let the kids go to third base and done nothing about it. Was I defiling their bodies? Was I serving them treats of the Devil? Sugary balls of pig fluff?

'I hate it when Muslims get caught up in trivialities,' said Ibrahim.

'Fine,' I said. 'But we take the secret of the origins of this marshmallow bag with us to the grave.'

'To the grave,' he said.

'Pinkie swear,' I said, holding out my hand.

'That's too forward,' he said.

'Can I tell the first story?' interrupted Musa.

Ibrahim was swiping a finger across his throat in an urgent manner. I wasn't sure if he was telling me to stop Musa or scratching an itch. Since he was always a little agitated, it was hard to tell. I went with itch.

'Sure,' I said. 'The scarier, the better.'

'In my grandmother's village in Pakistan, there's a jinn who sneaks into the houses at night when kids are sleeping in their beds,' Musa began.

'Is it easier to sneak in because the houses are made of cardboard?' asked Maria.

'Probably,' said Musa, not to be deterred. 'Plus the jinn had the ability to turn into a dog so no one would suspect it was a jinn.'

'How could you tell it wasn't just a dog?' asked Maria.

It was a fair question. But it didn't stymie Musa.

'Because one foot remained human. That was the way you could tell he wasn't a dog.'

I was starting to understand that maybe Ibrahim's neck hadn't been itchy.

'You could tell this jinn was coming when you heard the steps. The human foot dragged.'

The children gasped.

'What was it going to do to the children?' asked Maria.

'Jinn possess children so they become like them,' he said.

'What does "possess" mean?' asked a terrified Maria.

'It means that they take over your bodies and minds,' said Musa. 'But they can only do it at night when you go to sleep.'

'I don't want to sleep,' said Maria. There was murmuring among all the campers.

'Don't worry, jinn only come out in secluded areas,' said Musa.

'We're pretty secluded,' said Lumya.

'But they prefer secluded areas with graveyards,' said Musa. Everyone seemed to relax.

'There's a graveyard about a mile from here,' said Dwayne in a helpful tone.

Everyone looked petrified. Even Ibrahim looked a little sick. The children's paranoia had also infected me. We Muslims believe in the jinn. I suddenly wanted to be anywhere but here, and there was no way back to our cabins without travelling through the woods. I felt paralysed. I could see that the other campers had the same thought I did.

We couldn't stay by the campfire all night. Or could we?

We heard a sound. Steps and then a scraping noise.

'Oh, very funny, Ibrahim,' I said, trying to cut the tension. Jinn stories around the campfire always brought out the pranksters.

'It's not me,' said Ibrahim. He did a quick count of the campers.

'We're all here,' said Lumya. The sounds of the odd walking got louder.

Thump. Scrape. Thump. Scrape.

'How do you get rid of jinn?' asked Dwayne, looking a little whiter than usual.

'You say a prayer,' said Ibrahim. 'Which is it?'

'I think it's sura Baqarah,' said Lumya.

'No, that sura takes two hours to recite – we'll all be possessed by then.'

'*Salaam alaikum*, boys and girls,' bellowed a loud, Bob Marley-like voice.

There was Brother Abdullah, on crutches with his foot in bandages.

Ibrahim lunged at him in relief. All the horror of the last few minutes seeped out of me. I felt like jelly.

'Thank Allah you're here,' said Ibrahim.

'That's amazing,' said Dwayne. 'Muslims can turn dogs into human beings.'

'No, Muslims just get scared really easily,' I told Dwayne, disappointing him yet again.

With Abdullah's sudden appearance, the jinn stories were forgotten and we had the courage to make it back to the mess hall for hot chocolate.

'I thought you broke your foot?' I said.

'Turns out it was just a bad sprain,' said Abdullah.

'It's a sign from God that you came,' said Ibrahim.

'Yeah,' I said, agreeing with Ibrahim. 'God works in mysterious ways.'

'Not that mysterious,' said Abdullah. 'I got a phone call from a worried parent whose kid wanted to know if their grandmother was being swept away in a rainstorm and who then asked what a throbbing gristle was.'

'It's still a sign from God that we needed you,' said Ibrahim.

I felt insulted. 'No, it's a sign from God that we could use more support.'

It was a God-off.

'You two, just relax,' said Abdullah. 'No one knows what God's signs are except for God.'

The counsellors got the kids off to their cabins.

'So, are you having a good time?' asked Abdullah.

'Not really, but I think I've figured out what I have to do next with my life.'

'And what's that?'

'I was hoping to drop out of university because it's too hard, but I figure I have to finish what I started.'

'That's profound,' said Abdullah.

'It's why God sent me to this camp.'

'You volunteered,' corrected Abdullah.

I wanted to go back to figuring out Newton's laws. University was a cakewalk compared to the real world, which

I wasn't ready to join just yet. Camp hadn't exactly been a sign – more a whack to my head.

Abdullah smiled at me. 'As long as you're not hearing voices, it's all good.'

Medical School Reject

'What do you mean he has only one eye?' I heard my mother ask as I walked into the living room. 'His hobby? Hmm, I guess if you pull a fishing rod out of the water too quickly . . . Yes, that is an excellent salary though.'

'Ummi, what are you doing?' I hissed, incredulous.

'Finding you a husband,' said my mother, covering the phone with one hand.

'But—'

'Don't tell me that you have a prejudice against men with one eye, because that's not very Islamic, is it?'

'No, but—'

'One eye, two eyes, what does it matter as long as he has a good job? You don't have to go fishing with him. In fact, when you marry him, best to keep him on dry land. Accountants need at least one good eye.' She returned to her call.

Her enthusiastic search for a husband was my fault. It had started the moment I got my letter from the University of Toronto's med school. I read the first line – *We regret to inform*

you – and my life was over. Since the day I was born, the Life
Plan had been for me to be a doctor. Since I had been old
enough to know what a career was, I had been groomed to be
Dr Zarqa. Since I started learning, the aim was to get me into
medical school. Never mind that I passed out when we took
blood samples with a pipette to determine type. I just figured
I'd will myself to love haemoglobin, like some sort of med
school vampire. But what I couldn't do was will myself to
make sense of the byzantine world of science. Chemistry,
physics and calculus had been my undoing and left me with an
abysmal record that had failed to impress the med school selection committee: turns out it takes more than an immigrant
father's lifelong desire for his only daughter to become a doctor
to influence the admissions process. So when I opened that
letter, my life exploded. Life Plan A went up in smithereens.

But my mother had a Plan B.

'Let's get you married,' she said, happy that she could finally
interfere with my life properly. Her biggest fear was that too
much education might result in old, dried-up ovaries. My
father had so far squashed her matrimonial dreams for me,
because he believed marriage was for women who failed to get
into medical school.

I had officially become one of those.

My mother schemed while my father sulked. After a few
days of her phone calls, I felt desperate enough to do the
unthinkable – talk to her about my feelings. I walked into the
kitchen as she was adding water to wholewheat flour to make
dough for rotis. As she expertly kneaded the mixture with her
hands, I leaned against the counter.

'Ummi, I can't get married yet,' I said.

'Why not?' she asked as the mixture turned into a ball of
dough.

'I have to find myself.'

'You're standing right there. What's wrong with you?'

'I need to find a career,' I implored.

'Why can't you find one *after* you're married?'

'Because you of all people know how hard that is.'

My mother's hands stopped momentarily in the dough. When she was my age, her father didn't want her to further her education. In his world, only men needed to get educated, since they supported a family. Women stayed home and raised children, so only minimum schooling was necessary. My mother had wanted more. Her sisters, who had been married young, sympathized with her. They waited until their parents left for hajj, and then enrolled my mother in a boarding school in Murree, sixty kilometres north-east of Islamabad. After she completed her two years of teacher training, her marriage to my father was arranged quickly and she emigrated to England.

My mother's life became consumed with a new country, a new life and a new baby. Then, less than a year later, her parents died in a car crash on their way to a wedding. Our little family became her everything. She never had a chance to teach.

'My parents arranged my marriage,' retorted my mother. 'And it was the last thing they were able to do for me.'

It was hard to compete against such a tragedy.

'Please give me more time,' I said. 'It's really important to me.'

My mother stopped kneading again for a few seconds.

'Fine. I'll give you a few months to sort yourself out, but after that it's the one-eyed fisherman accountant.'

It was a reprieve.

They say education is never wasted, but I'd make an exception. Getting my BSc had been the most stultifyingly boring thing I had ever done. I had tried to pay attention during my science classes, but the formulas just didn't spark for me. I wrote the answer to the penultimate question in my final physics exam, where it asked me to calculate the internal surface area of a rotating cube, as:

Dear Physics People,

I'm sure there's a perfectly reasonable mathematical formula for solving this question. Here's the thing: I don't remember learning it. Don't take this personally. I'm sure you taught it. It's just that I have trouble absorbing things that make no sense. Don't you want to stare up at the stars and just enjoy them for what they truly are? I know they're just balls of burning gas to you, but they're also poetic and can cause people to fall in love and contemplate life. So I'm wondering if there's a way to make the calculation of the surface of a rotating cube more romantic. I think then I would be able to solve this problem.

Yours truly,

Zarqa Nawaz

My essay came back with a zero. There was a notation beside it: *You're terrible at physics. Have you considered being a writer?* But for me, the daughter of conservative Pakistani immigrants, a career such as a novelist, journalist or filmmaker was too sexy – like wearing fishnet stockings or sparkly eyeliner, things that good Muslim girls didn't do.

But desperate times called for un-Islamic measures. I scoured university calendars for professional schools. The applications for the tame options like teachers' college had passed. Only the deadline for Ryerson's School of Journalism in Toronto loomed, like a glittery, forbidden disco ball at the end of a dark tunnel.

I heard my mother on the phone.

'How did he lose the thumb? . . . High schools should really ban shop class . . . No, I didn't know you could use a big toe to replace it. Surgery has come a long way. Is his walking affected?'

I quickly filled out the form and mailed it.

A few weeks later, a letter arrived.

We are pleased to inform . . .

'What's that?' asked my mother.

'An interview for journalism school,' I said.

'How long is the programme?'

'Two years.' I could feel her do a quick calculation of my age in her head. 'Don't worry, my ovaries will still be fresh by the time I get out.'

'But you still have to get in,' she replied, returning to her Rolodex.

'What's wrong, dear? You don't look well,' said a well-meaning secretary.

I sat in the waiting room of Ryerson's Journalism Department with dark circles under my eyes. I had dreamed restlessly all night about fishing with the accountant. I had accidently jerked the line too hard and impaled his remaining good eye.

'There's a lot of competition to get into this programme, isn't there?'

'Oh yes, it's the best in the country,' she said. 'Students

have been putting together their résumés for years.'

A picture of me in a garish Indian wedding dress next to my beaming, triumphant mother flashed through my mind. I looked at the other student waiting with me.

'Do you know what they ask about during the interview?' I said.

'What you can bring to journalism that no one else can,' he replied.

Desperation, I thought. But I knew that wouldn't fly.

'I interviewed the Prime Minister for our Boy Scout newsletter.' He pulled out a photograph of his eight-year-old self standing with Prime Minister Joe Clark from a large portfolio of clippings from community newspapers.

I looked at the manila folder in my lap. I had a poster I had made for Muslim camp. It was colourful. Plus a column I wrote once about how to do ablution when there's no water. 'Don't underestimate dust.'

I was screwed. I flipped nervously through a copy of *Chatelaine*.

'Zarqa Nawaz,' said the secretary. 'You're next.'

I walked into an office with dark wooden bookcases and a squeaky floor. An elderly man with salt-and-pepper hair was seated behind an old metal desk. He stood up to greet me.

'I noticed that you have a science degree,' he said as I sat down.

'Is that a problem?' I asked. So screwed.

'We've never had a student apply with a BSc before. Our applicants usually have a BA.'

'I like to be different?' I offered.

'That's great. I thought you were going to tell me that you wanted to be a doctor and wound up here as second choice,' he said.

Only choice.

'I figured everybody studies English. Been there, done that. Why not study something totally unique? Bring a whole new perspective to journalism.'

'That's exactly what we're looking for,' he said happily.

'Really?'

'Tell me what you will bring to this programme from your degree that no one else can.'

My mind filled with useless information, like how to calculate the internal surface area of a rotating cube – why was that starting to make sense *now*?

'Most students just want to interview the Prime Minister,' he said.

'So typical,' I said. 'I prefer to impart knowledge that will be useful to humanity, help people in real ways. I want to change the face of journalism.'

'Can you tell me one thing that you learned about in school that would make a useful contribution to society?'

My mind fell back to the magazine I had read in the waiting area before I came in.

'Did you know there's a new contraceptive on the market called Norplant?' I said.

'No, what's that?'

'It's a device that is infused with hormones and put in a woman's arm. It releases contraception for five years so a woman doesn't have to remember to take the Pill every day.' I prayed his wife was already menopausal.

'That's amazing. I've never heard of it.'

'Good – I mean, of course not. Information about it hasn't been published yet,' I said. 'I learned about it in my physics class.'

'Really? How strange. Well, it's a travesty that more people don't know about it,' he said. 'I'm sure women's magazines would be very interested.'

'Yes, they would be. Are you an . . . err . . . avid reader of women's magazines?'

'No, I stick to hunting magazines. My wife passed away a year ago so I cancelled all the subscriptions.'

'Thank God . . . I mean, she's gone back to God. I'm a bit religious, in case you didn't notice,' I said, quickly pointing at my headscarf. 'In fact, I should be praying soon. Which way is north-east?'

It had just occurred to me that having a dead wife didn't necessarily mean he wasn't knowledgeable about contraceptives. What if he was seeing someone younger? She could out me.

'You're not dating anyone right now, are you?' I asked.

He looked at me oddly. 'No, since my wife passed, I've devoted my life to keeping her memory alive.'

'It's just that my mother's single and I thought you might be available,' I said, suddenly realizing the implication of my question and trying to divert him from thinking I was hitting on him, but that was an even worse idea, since my mother wasn't single and, even if she was, would never consider dating, never mind marrying, a white guy.

'Thanks for your concern, but I'm fine,' he said. 'I think you'd be a fantastic asset to our programme, what with your knowledge of the latest trends in reproductive technology.'

I was in! But then my no-nonsense journalism instructor announced on my first day that I would need to find an out-of-town job placement.

'Forget it,' said my mother. 'You're not going anywhere.'

'Why not?' I said. 'It's part of my programme to do a practical component.'

'Do it in Toronto.'

'But it's impossible to get hired in Toronto while you're in college. They're looking for people who already have regional experience. I have to go somewhere regional.'

'It's forbidden in Islam for an unmarried woman to leave home,' said my mother.

'No it's not. Where does it say that?'

'In the Qur'an.'

'It's not in the Qur'an. Show me, if you're so sure.'

'Fine, I read it somewhere else.'

'Where?'

'That's not important,' said my mother. 'The point is, you're not leaving home unless you get married. People will talk. "She left home and who knows what she did while she was gone?"'

Ah, the real problem.

'But you left home,' I countered.

'And it nearly broke their hearts,' said my mother. 'They were worried about my reputation. It's difficult for girls to get married if their reputations are ruined.'

'Why does marriage have to be my end goal?'

'Because you'll be lonely after I die.'

'At least I'll have a job.'

My mother wouldn't budge.

I called the local paper, hoping for a miracle.

'*Oakville Beaver*,' said a disgruntled voice.

'Hi, I'm a journalism student from Ryerson, and I wanted to know if you're accepting interns.'

'Not really,' he said. 'We don't have the budget.'

'I could bring knowledge to your paper that no one else can,' I said, desperate.

'Like what?' he asked.

'Ever heard of Norplant?'

'Yeah, my girlfriend uses it.'

'Do you know how to calculate the internal surface area of a rotating cube?'

He hung up on me.

My life was over. Again.

I sat with my head in my hands. The phone rang and my mother answered.

'Really, he can crack his wrists and get out of handcuffs!' said my mother. 'No, thank you. Even we have standards.'

Then Saddam Hussein invaded Kuwait and my life started again. With the Gulf War I realized I had an advantage in my classroom. Because Muslims were too busy trying to get into medical school, I was the sole representative of my people in the class.

I decided to be strategic and write an article about how the Canadian Broadcasting Corporation's main news programme, *The National*, was covering the Gulf War.

Playing on the good will of the journalism community for student reporters, I booked an interview with David Bazay, *The National*'s producer.

'You're a student at Ryerson?' asked David as I made myself comfortable in his office just off the main hub of the news department.

'Yes,' I replied, trying to look authoritative. 'I'm concerned about how your reporters are covering the Gulf War.'

'What are you concerned about?' he asked worriedly. I had no idea. I just wanted a job.

'Do you think a Muslim woman in hijab could ever be hired as an on-air television reporter?' I asked. 'Because then for sure it wouldn't look like you were discriminating.'

He looked at me with interest. 'Once I wore a toque

while I was delivering a news report on camera. My producer told me to lose it or I'd be gonzo,' he told me matter-of-factly.

I took that as a no. 'So I couldn't do the weekend report?'

'Have you got any regional experience?' he asked. 'Because we hire from the CBC outposts. Have you considered moving up north?'

I couldn't tell him my mother wouldn't let me. I needed another strategy. 'Did that reporter just pronounce "Muslim" as "moozlim"?' I asked, watching a news report on the monitor in his office.

'That's not how you pronounce it?'

'No, he's pronouncing the first part like "mooing", as in a cow,' I said as confidently as I could. 'Pronounce it like the "puss" in "pussy cat".'

'That's fascinating,' said David. 'I didn't know we were pronouncing these terms incorrectly.'

'And you're mispronouncing Tariq Aziz as well.' Tariq Aziz was Saddam Hussein's right-hand dude. 'The second syllable shouldn't sound like "reek" as in smells bad. It should sound like "rick" as in "Rick Astley".'

I looked around the newsroom. There wasn't a lot of diversity, so there wasn't anyone around to challenge my authority on how to pronounce things properly. David called in his secretary.

'Yvette is a Christian Arab,' he explained. 'She can tell me if you're right.'

I said 'Muslim' and 'Tariq Aziz' for her.

'She knows how to pronounce words,' said Yvette. 'So what?'

David sat down and scratched his head.

'How would you like a part-time job?'

'Done. Should I wear a red scarf? I think it would help my head pop on camera.'

'You're not going on camera, but this is what I want,' said David. 'This war is gonna take a while and we need to know more about the make-up of the Muslim community in Canada.'

He gave me a job to come up with a detailed report, and I spent my Christmas holidays researching. It wasn't the sexy journalism job I had hoped for, but I figured even Bob Woodward and Carl Bernstein had to start somewhere.

'So how is the job hunt going?' asked No-nonsense Instructor when we got back from our holidays. Other students had secured jobs as reporters in far-flung areas of various provinces.

'That's not a real journalism job,' he said when I told him what I'd landed. 'A reporter is not someone who writes reports. Find a real one or else.'

I went back to David.

'We appreciated your report,' he said. 'Very useful for the reporters.'

'Which I'm not allowed to be.'

'Not unless you're willing to first move north to Nunavut,' he said.

'I have an allergy to polar bears,' I said. 'The fur sends me into anaphylactic shock. Do you have any jobs in the newsroom?'

He mulled it over.

'We have the weekend night shift for *Newsworld*,' he said. 'No one ever wants that.'

'What's that?'

'We hire people to monitor the news feeds and summarize key stories for the night reporter.'

'But I'd be writing the news?' I asked.

'Yep.'

I was saved.

'You're working in the middle of the night?' asked my mother.

'Ummi, I go into work at 8 p.m. and work until 8 a.m.,' I said. 'It's perfectly safe.'

'Fine,' she said. 'Do not walk around downtown Toronto at 2 a.m. People might talk.'

My friend Janice, whom I'd met at Ryerson, worked the weekend overnight shifts with me. We read the news feeds and summarized the most important stories. But our biggest responsibility was to wake David if something major happened in the world. There was a rumour circulating around the CBC that when Saddam Hussein invaded Kuwait, the night attendants hadn't thought it was a big enough news story to wake the news executives. They were fired. Needless to say, the two of us were nervous about missing another big story.

'North Korea just stationed troops near the border with South Korea,' said Janice.

'What would happen if North Korea attacked South Korea?' I asked her.

'World War Three,' she said. 'Or maybe nothing.'

I couldn't afford to lose this job. I called.

'Hello,' said David's groggy voice on the other end.

'Sir, North Korea has troops on South Korea's border,' I said.

'Have they attacked?' he asked.

'No, they're just massed at the border,' I replied.

'They do that all the time,' said David. 'Don't call me unless they attack. And, Zarqa?'

'Yes?' I said, worried about his tone of voice.

'That rumour you heard was just a rumour. If something

serious happens, one of our bureaus will call us. So please don't
call me again or you'll be gonzo.'

Needless to say I was pretty woozy in my editing class on
Monday mornings. It was a detail-oriented class and I just
didn't have the attention span after staying up all night on
Sundays fretting about North Koreans. The instructor pulled
me aside.

'Your marks are abysmal,' he said.

'Yeah, I'm a little tired in class,' I said.

'I'm afraid I can't pass you.'

'What? You're flunking me out of journalism school?'

'We're putting you on academic probation. We'll watch
your grades and see how you're doing in other subjects.'

'So as long as I pass everything else, I'll be OK?'

'You'll have to take the editing class a second time,' he said.
'We have standards to maintain.'

When I got home that evening, I must have looked pensive.

'What's wrong?' asked my mother as she chopped onions.

'I failed editing class.'

'But you're not going to fail journalism school?'

'As long as I pass the second time, I'll be OK.'

'So smarten up.'

I was surprised. I thought she'd pull out her old wedding
dress to see if it would fit me.

'My parents came to visit me when I was in teachers' college,' said my mother as she slid the onions into a frying pan.
'My father came to pull me out. But when my mother saw
how happy I was, she insisted that I be allowed to finish.' It was
as close as my mother had ever come to understanding me.
'Journalism school suits you,' she said. 'You're much happier
there than when you were doing your BSc.'

'Is the one-eyed fisherman accountant going to wait?'

'Oh, he got married. The good ones always go quickly.'

'Well, there's always more fish in the sea,' trying to lighten the mood.

'Remember, a career can't replace companionship,' she said as she added cumin to the sizzling onions. 'I just pray that I can get you married before I die.'

Always the tragic backdrop.

I passed editing the second time around and thrived in journalism school. My grades suddenly went from Cs to As. And I even won an award for one of my stories.

When I told the head of the department, he said, 'Good. Now we don't have to kick you out.'

Then I saw the man who had interviewed me for admission. 'I remember you,' he said. 'I heard you're doing really well.'

'Thanks,' I replied, a little nervous.

'By the way, I found out about Norplant,' he said.

'Oh, did you start dating a younger woman?'

'No, I have a daughter who's on it,' he said. 'She had a pretty good laugh when I told her about this "new" discovery of yours. She's had it in her arm for about a year.'

'Sorry about that,' I said sheepishly. 'I didn't know how else to impress you. I never had a chance to interview the Prime Minister when I was growing up.'

'You really did want to be a doctor, didn't you?'

'More than anything else in the world,' I replied. 'But when that didn't work out my mother got fixated on getting me married. She's a little old-fashioned. She believes that marriage is the most important thing in your life. I think she's insane.'

'No, your mother's right,' said the professor. 'My wife is the reason my life was worth living. Don't discount your mother's advice.'

'So you're not angry with me for lying?'

'Half of journalism is bullshitting to get stories,' he said. 'You need to be creative in this business to get ahead.'

'Thanks for not ratting me out,' I replied.

'No problem. But I do have one favour to ask.'

'What's that?' I said with trepidation.

'I'm looking to start dating again. What's your mother's number?'

I looked aghast. 'She doesn't date white men. She doesn't consider white people marriage material.'

'I'm sure I could change her mind.'

'Plus you'd have to convert and become Muslim.'

'It's an interesting faith,' he said. 'I'm agnostic but I'm willing to give Islam a try. Could I call her?'

'She's actually not a widow,' I confessed. 'My parents have been married for over twenty years, more or less happily. I don't think my dad would take a call from you well. And my mother even less so. No offence.'

'None taken,' he said. 'I was just pulling your leg. I figure now we're even for the Norplant hoax. So, how are you liking journalism?'

'I love it. I didn't think I had a future until now.'

'It's the most exciting career in the world, isn't it?'

'Like fishnet stockings,' I said.

Sami

Muzammal wanted to marry Suzanne. My brother might as well have said that he wanted to marry a lemur.

'Birds of a feather flock together,' said my father, stunned.

'But we're different birds from you guys,' Muzammal replied.

In my parents' universe, there had never been a marriage outside of our extended Punjabi tribe. Tribal marriages were sacred. Suzanne's Scottish background might be tribal in its own way, but it just didn't register for my parents. Nevertheless, Muzammal believed that the Scottish and Punjabi highlands were destined to mesh, come hell or high water.

Hell first.

But my mother immediately recognized a strategic opportunity. For years she had been wringing her hands, watching my singular obsession with becoming the next star on television news. I wasn't taking her marriage concerns seriously enough. She needed an ally, and who better than Muzammal?

'Your sister must be married first. You know that.'

He didn't know that.

In Pakistan, a sister always marries before a brother, even if he's older, otherwise rumours spread throughout the village. The sister's damaged goods. She must have six toes on one foot or a horribly hairy back or, perhaps worse, the genetic malady of speaking her mind.

'But we live in Oakville, not Faisalabad. No one thinks that way any more,' argued Muzammal.

No one except my mother and all her friends, and that was enough. Until I got married, no one else could get married to anyone, brown or white.

Even my youngest brother, Muddaththir, who was just turning eighteen, started to worry.

'Am I going to have to wait too?' he asked.

'Yes,' said my mother.

'But she might take forever to unload,' he said. 'She's kind of weird.'

'There's a man out there who will believe that's an attractive quality,' said my mother. And then, tying all our fates together: 'Find him.'

Cornered by a traditional mother and two desperate, single brothers.

It wasn't that I didn't want to get married. I did. The idea of a husband who loved me for exactly who I was appealed to me. My idea was that I'd meet him while working as a journalist and win him over with my personality. However, even though I had now graduated I needed to gain experience by working in a regional location. But my mother wouldn't let me leave home till I got married. Her fear was that I'd get so obsessed with my career that I'd never try to find a partner. So she wouldn't let me have one without the other.

'Ummi, what am I supposed to tell prospective employers?' I said, frustrated at her obtuseness.

'Ask them if they know any good Muslim men,' said my mother. 'And you need to try flirting.' Coming from my mother, this was rich. My mom used to insist that flirting was forbidden in Islam, a sin on a par with rape, murder and pillage. I'd never been able to find that verse in the Qur'an, but my mother insisted you had to read between the lines. Advice about seduction from a mother who had an arranged marriage and who believed flirting was heinous showed her desperation.

'And smiling,' she said. 'Work on your small-talk.'

'Like what?' I asked.

'Ask them where they buy their prayer mats from,' she said.

Both my parents firmly believed in arranged marriage. That was why they were still together after twenty-five years. 'All this talking and getting to know each other for a love marriage. And what happens? You're still disappointed. If you have an arranged marriage, you don't call it disappointment, you call it a husband.'

'How could you marry someone you never saw before?' I asked her. It just boggled my mind.

'That's the way things were back then,' she said. 'Love comes afterwards.'

'Why can't love come first?' I asked.

'White people fall in love beforehand,' said my mother, 'and they still get divorced. So one method isn't superior to the other.' I had a suspicion that she felt her method was superior.

I couldn't get a real and permanent job, Muzammal couldn't get married, and my mother couldn't get any sleep. Famous newscasters never had this problem.

My parents feverishly worked their circle of family friends

to find the perfect husband. They insisted he come from the Punjab, a narrow area of Pakistan. They wanted to cement ties back home, and I was their mortar. Then suddenly they hit a rich vein of Punjabi men who lived in the United States, who were completing PhDs and needed landed-immigrant status with a Canadian bride attached to it. I had morphed into a citizenship with benefits.

One day I came home from CBC, where I was working on a freelance radio project, and slumped on to a chair in the kitchen. There were samosas on the table, an unexpected treat. As I snatched one, I noticed my mother looking me up and down.

'What?' I asked.

'Maybe you should put on some good clothes,' said my mother.

'To eat samosas? They don't really care how I look.'

She shifted awkwardly in her seat.

'There's a nice man in the living room.'

'In the living room? Now?' An ambush. I jumped to my feet, looking for an exit.

'He's the son of my father's brother's nephew's friend from college,' said my mother. 'He's here for some tea.' She shoved a tray into my hands and pushed me out to the living room. Clearly my outfit was good enough.

Sitting on the brown floral couch was a brown guy dressed in a black suit who was obviously just as nervous as I was. I smiled at him awkwardly as I poured him some tea. We sat silently sipping together. It was excruciating.

'So, where do you buy your prayer mats?'

'Pakistan,' he said. 'Isn't that where everyone gets them?'

I smiled. I was flirting!

'What did you study?' he asked.

'Journalism,' I replied.

'That's nice. So your parents told you about the condition?' he asked, munching nervously on a samosa.

'What condition?'

'I have to live in Pakistan for a few years after I finish my PhD.'

'What's that got to do with me?' I asked, not making the connection.

'Of course you'd have to live in Karachi too.'

Oh.

I tried to imagine working for the *Karachi Herald*. Might it count as a regional paper?

As I listened to the awkward buzz of the heating vent, I wondered if there was any chemistry between us. Maybe he was perfect for me but I didn't know it? Marriage would end so many of my problems in one fell swoop. I went into the kitchen and told my mother I thought I could make it work. After all, she'd had to move out of the country she loved, so why not me? She was thrilled. I went back into the living room with a tray of cookies.

'So you don't have a problem with moving to Pakistan?'

'We go where God sends us,' I said.

'I don't really believe in God,' he replied.

Wait a minute.

'What do you mean?'

'I mean, Islam is an old and venerated faith; but I prefer science over religion.'

I excused myself, went to the kitchen and told my mother I was wrong. I couldn't marry him.

'Why not?' said my mother. 'You two were getting along so well.'

'He doesn't believe in God,' I replied.

My mother went quiet. Although we had radically different opinions on our faith, we intersected on one issue.

'Fine,' said my mother with difficulty. 'At the very least, we want a husband who believes in a higher power. We'll vet them more carefully next time. Who knew that Muslims could also be atheists?'

So began an endless blur of young Pakistani men studying at American schools. They came so frequently and left so quickly that I refused to learn their names, and would refer to them only by their state of origin. Ohio didn't want children. Wisconsin wasn't willing to have a wife who worked. Louisiana didn't want to work himself. Utah came highly recommended through my mother's friend's halal butcher's second cousin but showed up smelling distinctly of whisky.

Every so often I would get my hopes up. California was sitting in the living room when I walked in one Saturday afternoon. His name was Adil and he was cute, like a young, brown Paul McCartney. He had grown up in Pakistan and was doing a PhD in a science-related field at Stanford University.

'I've been staring at you my entire life,' he said.

I had visited Pakistan when I was five years old and wound up in a photograph with his elder brother, who had just graduated from high school. That photo hung in their family home.

I was smitten in all of five minutes. It was obviously a sign from God. I was being rewarded for having taken the scenic route through America's heartland with stoic grace. Now a romantic, good-looking man from California was being handed to me on a silver platter.

We talked about different subjects, and then we came to religion.

'I believe in the Qur'an but not hadith,'* he said.

Not again.

'But you have to believe in hadith,' I said, confused.

'I don't,' he said. 'They turn faith into endless rules.'

I liked those rules. They had given me structure. They had helped me torture my parents.

'That's crazy,' I said. 'You can't do that.'

Apparently he could.

Where was God when you needed a miracle?

'I might have found someone,' Muzammal said. He looked more relieved than me. I had forgotten what my obtuseness was costing him. Through my brother's network of friends he had heard about a young medical student named Sami Haque.

That name rang a bell. When I was at university, I would travel from Toronto on the occasional weekend to visit my best friend, Rahat, who was studying at Queen's University in Kingston. Rahat's roommate, Sabreena, kept a photo of her brother Sami on the corkboard. I remembered I had stared at the handsome young man, who looked like he was staring straight back at me. But he'd been engaged to someone.

Recently I had heard from Rahat that the engagement had ended. However Sami lived in Saskatchewan, a few provinces and another universe away from me. I had no idea how to reach him. Somehow Sami had found a way to reach me. The feeling of hope came back – even when Muzammal told me that Sami was completing a family-medicine residency way up north in La Ronge, which was thirteen hours north of the Canadian/American border, just south of the 60th parallel.

---

*Hadith are a collection of sayings and observed actions of the Prophet that number in the thousands.

Sami had been born in Montreal to Bengali parents who had immigrated to Canada in the 1960s, and he had grown up on the prairies. His parents had left finding a wife up to him.

I decided it was the miracle I had prayed for.

'I want to marry him,' I said. He was The One.

Now someone just had to convince Sami.

Muzammal was a little startled but wasn't about to question Providence. He sent out a message through the network that Sami could come and visit.

Sami phoned our house one evening when my parents were out.

'My name is Sami,' said a very deep voice.

'This is Zarqa,' I replied.

Awkward silence.

'Should I be talking to your brother?' he asked.

'He's not home,' I replied. 'But I am.'

'Are you OK with talking?'

'Sure,' I said.

'I've heard a lot about you.'

The words were like an arrow straight into my heart. No one I had met during the last few torturous months had ever said that to me. I felt my face flush. He had heard about me. And he was still calling.

'Really?' was all I could manage.

'You're a journalist. That's different. Everyone's always trying to become a doctor these days. Like me, I guess!' He laughed in that deep voice of his. 'I think you'd be an interesting person to meet.'

'Sure,' I said. I could be interesting. 'So you live in Saskatchewan? Is that one or two provinces over from Ontario?'

There was a moment of silence.

'So it's true what they say about people from Toronto,' he said. 'You guys are oblivious to the rest of the country.'

After another silence, during which I strongly considered asking him about his prayer mat, he finally spoke.

'So what are you up to these days?'

'I've been looking for a job, but it seems that I'm going to need to leave the city for somewhere more remote. But, you know . . . that's hard right now.' 'Because I have to get married first' was what I wanted to say, but I managed to keep that to myself.

'There's a CBC station up here,' he offered quietly.

'Yeah, I checked,' I said. 'It's above a general store.' But we both knew that I couldn't just pack up and work in that station. We'd have to decide about each other first.

'I'd like to come and meet you,' he said.

'How soon can you get here?' I said.

He laughed. 'I'm doing my residency, so I don't have much flexibility. But I have a break at Thanksgiving, which is in ten weeks.'

'*Ten weeks!*' I yelled. 'That's too long.'

I was lucky he didn't hang up then and there. 'I'm serious, I can't come sooner,' he replied.

'Fine,' I said, simultaneously disappointed and excited. He was definitely The One. I knew I had been wrong before, but this time it all added up.

'Any other questions?' he asked tentatively.

'Do you believe in God?'

'Of course, I'm Muslim.'

'You'd be surprised,' I answered.

When my mother came home that evening, she too was excited.

'Uncle Mumtaz found a man doing his PhD in Nebraska. He's perfect for you. He has a good job and doesn't mind a wife who works occasionally. He may even be willing to settle somewhere in North America,' she told me, unpacking groceries. My father, sitting in the kitchen with us, tried not to make eye contact with me.

'He's coming to meet you in two weeks,' she went on.

'I have news too,' I said. 'I talked to Sami, a guy Muzammal found, and I think he's The One, so I don't need to meet your Nebraska after all.'

'But Uncle Mumtaz will be insulted after all the work he did for us,' said my mother. Since Uncle Mumtaz was not really an uncle but a friend of the family, I wasn't worried.

'I don't want to meet Nebraska; I know Saskatchewan – I mean, Sami – is going to work out.'

'Listen to me, two men are better than one,' my mother called over her shoulder as she left the kitchen. 'Meet them both and then see who still wants to marry you.'

I knew I'd need to get my father on side to get out of meeting Nebraska. It was going to be difficult. He'd never warmed up to the topic of marriage. He didn't mind if I stayed single, and I imagined he wouldn't have too many qualms if my brothers were forced to join the priesthood. At seven on Saturday morning, when I knew he'd be the only one up, I spoke to him.

'Daddy, I know it was just one phone call, but I really think Sami's going to work out.'

'Isn't he the one who lives in the Arctic?'

'It's still closer than Pakistan,' I countered.

'OK,' laughed my father, 'I'll tell Uncle Mumtaz that Nebraska can't come.'

I thought that was the end of it but I should have known

better. For my parents, truth is a moving object. My father told Uncle Mumtaz that his mother was unwell in Pakistan and he had to rush back to be with her. By unwell, he meant dead and he was going to visit the grave, but why split hairs?

Unfortunately Nebraska had bought a non-refundable ticket and couldn't cancel his flight. 'Just meet Nebraska,' said my mother. 'How do you know that Saskatchewan will work out?'

Because you didn't have anything to do with him, I thought, but 'I feel that this is who God would want me to marry' is what I said.

'I feel that Nebraska is who God would want you to marry,' said my mother. 'So let's meet both and find out who God really wants.'

Again with the God-off.

My mother wouldn't relent, so Muzammal brokered a deal for me. I'd only have to meet with Nebraska for five minutes. Five minutes.

'And I want to meet him at Uncle Mumtaz's house, and I don't want you around.'

Surprisingly, my mother agreed.

Two weeks later, Muzammal and I walked into Uncle Mumtaz's meticulously decorated house. I could see a polished pair of black shoes by the door. Their owner sat on a black leather sofa flanked by identical coffee tables with Chinese vases. Nebraska was slender, with short hair parted on the side and a kind face – which I avoided looking at.

'How are you?' I asked the Chinese vase.

Four minutes and fifty-two seconds to go.

'I'm fine,' he said.

'Good,' I said to the other Chinese vase.

'I'm very happy to meet you,' he said.

'So, where do you buy your prayer mats from?' I asked.

Four minutes and thirty-three seconds.

'Isn't everything made in China these days?' he replied.

'That's smart. They really do make the best ones.'

Awkward pause.

Four minutes and ten seconds left but I thought, Forget it.

'Well, have a good trip back to Nebraska.' I got up to leave.

Nebraska was flabbergasted. 'What? You're leaving already? Don't you want to talk some more?'

'Not really,' I said as I left the living room.

'Would you like a samosa?' asked a confused Uncle Mumtaz.

'Sure,' I said as I grabbed a samosa and put it in my pocket. 'I'll take it for the road.'

Uncle Mumtaz's wife looked at me as if I were insane. 'But the tea is—'

I never did find out what the tea was doing because I flew out the door.

The meeting was three minutes and fifty seconds shorter than the agreed time but I had feelings for someone else, and this meeting felt like adultery. My parents offered to drive Nebraska back to the airport (my father's mother having made a miraculous recovery).

'It isn't the money,' Nebraska apparently agonized and shouted for the entire ride, 'it's my time.'

He was in the middle of his PhD and couldn't afford unnecessary delays. My mother came home a wreck.

'Marry anyone,' she said. 'We don't care any more.'

I asked my parents to leave the house when Sami came over for the first time. Exhausted from their recent public humiliation,

they agreed. Muzammal bought us an apple pie, in the hope
that it would encourage romance and because his marriage to
Suzanne depended on it. My life, which was in a state of pur-
gatory, depended upon it. Sami had no idea how much hinged
on his very existence.

The doorbell rang and I heard Muzammal leading Sami into
the living room. My heart stopped beating. My brother found
me cowering in the kitchen.

'You've been through enough of these,' said Muzammal.
'You're an old hand at this.'

'It's scary when you think it might work out,' I said.

'Tell me about it,' he said as he pushed me out of the
kitchen.

As I walked towards the living room, I could see a pair of
raggedy, tattered running shoes sitting on the front hall mat.
Sami put down the newspaper he had been reading. He had
a round jovial face, a closely shaved beard flecked with red,
long flowing hair to his shoulders, the build of a rugby player
and pillowy lips. It was his mouth that caught my attention
right away. Wearing a smiley-face T-shirt with a pair of faded
blue jeans, he was the most exotic thing I had ever seen. He
was different from all the other brown men I had met. In fact,
he wasn't even very brown. He didn't seem to even notice the
difference in our colour. Like so many other cultures, South
Asians put a premium on fair-skinned women, and I knew that
would be true for his culture, Bengalis, too. It wasn't common
for a man to seek out a darker woman.

'So, we finally meet,' he said in that rich, deep voice of his.
I took my eyes away from his lips to meet his gaze.

'Finally,' I said, thinking about the ten weeks I had waited.

Muzammal came in with some apple pie on a plate and gave
me an arch look as he left the room.

'My uncle works at the CBC,' said Sami. 'Did you really tell the producer how to pronounce "Muslim"?'

Oh God.

'Well, I wanted to impress him so he'd give me a job,' I pleaded. 'I hope that isn't my legacy to the world of journalism.'

We talked about his career aspirations and life on the prairies.

I had heard enough. I wanted to get this show on the road.

'So, what should we do next?' I asked in what I hoped was a delicate manner.

'We should take our time and get to know each other.'

'How much time?' I answered, trying to keep desperation at bay.

'My next holiday is in December,' he said. 'We can talk some more then.'

I was starting to see my mother's point about the beauty and efficiency of arranged marriages. All this yammering, getting-to-know-you stuff was exhausting.

At this point my parents came home. My mother took one look at Sami and pulled me into the kitchen.

'His hair's too long!' she said nervously as she made tea to soothe her apprehension. She was used to clean-cut men in three-piece suits, eager to please her. A few years ago, Sami would have never made it to the living-room couch. However, now I was twenty-six and all the birds of that feather had flown; she was down to a guy who looked like a beach bum.

'Should I ask him to leave?' I replied, knowing that her sense of pragmatism would set in and that she knew this one wouldn't scream at them all the way to the airport.

I went back into the living room.

*

Sami and I talked every week on the phone until he came back in December. We went to the CBC, where I was working, together and I recorded a radio segment for the show *Morningside*. Afterwards we went to Pizza Hut for lunch. It was the first time we were alone without my parents hovering over us.

'We've talked a lot about your career, but how do you feel about family?'

'I'd like kids,' I said.

'Me too. How many do you want?' he asked.

'Depends. How many do you want?'

'Four.'

'Good round number, I like it. Four it is,' I replied.

Things were going well. I could hear the wedding bells chiming. I felt comfortable and easy around him.

'Are there other things you'd like me to know about you?' he asked.

I thought hard. 'I'm a very light sleeper. Any sound will wake me up.'

'Oh, I'm a pretty heavy sleeper,' he answered. 'Plus I snore a lot.'

'Hmmm . . . I get cold easily,' I said.

'I'm always hot. I love air-conditioning.'

We looked at each other. Suddenly things were not adding up. I was scrambling for common ground. 'I don't drink a lot of water,' I said.

'I drink water by the barrel,' he replied.

'We seem really different,' I said.

'It's a recipe for disaster,' said Sami as he took my glass of water and finished it. The bells had stopped ringing.

'You think so?' I asked, frightened.

'You're a strange person,' he said. 'A little spinny, too.'

'That's what people say,' I agreed sadly.

'I have a holiday coming up in May, Victoria Day.'

'More talking?' I asked wearily.

Sami rubbed his stubbled chin thoughtfully. 'No,' he said.

That was a marriage proposal if I had ever heard one.

But he was proposing to the wrong person. So when we got home, Sami asked my father whether he might marry me.

Turned out that Sami was also the wrong person to do the proposing.

'In our culture, children do not speak to parents about marriage,' said my father.

'So who should speak to you about this marriage?' asked Sami.

'Your father,' said my father.

'You know, my parents didn't even ask me if I wanted to get married,' said my father, reminiscing. He had been working as a structural engineer in England, sending money home to support his family, when his parents lured him back.

'I rushed home thinking my father was dying, and the band started to play at the airport.'

'It was the happiest day of his life,' said my mother. 'He just didn't realize it.'

My father said, 'Young people today have it so easy. You see each other before marriage. Sometimes get to know one another.'

'Not that much actually,' said Sami. 'So we're all good?'

'No,' said my father.

'What?' said my mother.

My father looked at me. 'You should reapply to medical school. You could still get in.'

Some dreams apparently never die.

'But *I'm* a doctor,' said Sami.

'You're the strangest-looking doctor I've ever seen,' sighed my father, who had obviously not been paying enough attention to this suitor.

'Yeah, I'm not big on dressing up, but I will graduate in May.'

'Well, at least he'll have a job,' said my mother, still eyeing his hair.

'And two eyes,' I added.

'What?' said Sami.

'Nothing,' I replied.

Sami flew back to Saskatchewan and asked his parents to fly to Toronto to meet mine. The meeting went well. The Pakistanis and the Bengalis had fought a war in 1972, but those bitter memories were going to end in this union. The wedding date was set: 22 May 1993, seven months after we'd met.

We got married in Taric Mosque in Toronto. I wore a cream *lehenga* accented with pearls and gold embroidery, and Sami wore a black suit. I was supposed to buy him a tie, but I forgot so his uncle lent him a burgundy bow tie. Sami looked like a waiter.

In South Asian custom, the bride is supposed to be sad because she's leaving her parents, so she cries a lot and acts like her wedding is a funeral. But I couldn't fake it. I acted like a Western bride and beamed at everybody, which made my mom feel that I was thwarting her culture. She kept swatting me to remind me to stop looking so happy, and I kept swatting back. We looked like we were killing mosquitoes on each other's arms. Between swats, I looked at my mother. She seemed both tired and elated. It had been a long journey for us both. There were days when I thought she was ruining my life with her obsession with marriage. But her obstinacy had paid off and I was marrying the one man who was right for me. Turning to watch Sami laughing, I knew I wouldn't have found him without my mother.

Muzammal and Suzanne were married four months later.

Birds of a different feather had come together.

How to Name a Muslim Baby

'What do you think of the name Maysa?' I asked my mother.

'I don't like it. Call her Munzal.'

'What? Munzal's a horrible name,' I said, flabbergasted. 'Why don't you like Maysa?'

'It's not Islamic.'

I was nine months pregnant with our first child. Sami and I had scoured all the halal butchers for every Muslim baby book we could get our hands on. (That was the only place you could buy them back then.) We had started our search for the perfect name the moment I knew I was pregnant. One name stood out to us: Maysa. Meaning 'a woman who walks with pride'. There was no second choice. We didn't even know at the time that we were going to have a girl. If we had had a boy, I guess he would have toddled with womanly pride. My mother's declaration devastated me.

'How Islamic is Zarqa?' said my father.

'It's very Islamic,' countered my mother. 'Lots of Muslims choose it.'

'Nobody had heard of Zarqa before you chose it,' said my father.

I had hated my name growing up. It was a really odd name, even for Muslims.

The only other Zarqa I ever met was when I was ten, and she was a sad-faced girl who looked like she couldn't believe her fate either. And that was it, except for the henna brand called Zarqa sold in my local halal butcher. (Yes, halal butchers.)

My mother had chosen my name because when she was pregnant she read a story about Zarqa al-Yamama, a legendary Arab woman of ancient times who was able to see great distances. Because she could see so well, she would warn her tribe when danger was approaching. Word of her powers got out, so one day the enemy tribe hid behind tree branches and when Zarqa warned her people that the forest was moving, they laughed at her. As a result, the enemy was able to defeat Zarqa's people. They then plucked out her eyes with the ancient culinary equivalent of a melon baller so that they could never be used in battle again. It was a pretty gruesome story.

'Why did that name appeal to her?' I asked my father.

'The problem is that your mother's name was so common. There were at least four Parveens in all of her classes growing up.'

My mother had been searching for a unique name, just like I was now. 'Fine. But Ummi, Zarqa's story predates Islam. Which means that she wasn't even Muslim, so how Muslim could my name be?'

'She didn't even exist,' said my father. 'She's just a legend, and one that's in almost all cultures.'

'Jordan named a city after her,' retorted my mother. 'So she could have existed. It is a beautiful name – you were lucky to grow up with a name that didn't sound like any of the others.'

Somehow, as a child, I forgot to feel lucky.

'It didn't sound like any of the names at school, but every time I watched TV as a kid, there was a creature from outer space who had a variation of my name, such as Zarkon or Zirkonian,' I complained.

'I can't help what white people do,' said my mother. 'They take perfectly good names and ruin them.'

But it wasn't just white people who had a problem with my name. Zarqa means 'blue'. Zarqa al-Yamama was named for her beautiful blue eyes. So for Arabs, the name Zarqa is synonymous with blue eyes.

'It's like my face is a disappointment to every Arab Muslim I meet. It's false advertising – my eyes are brown.'

'I didn't know then that it meant "blue",' said my mother. 'I thought it meant "brave woman".'

Pakistanis have a bad habit of picking Arabic names without understanding their meanings. Sometimes they open the Qur'an and plunk their finger down on a word and take that name for their child. I have known a Fig Tree, and a Table. Both were lovely people, considering.

One summer at camp, I met a guy named Ahmer, which means 'red'. We were teased about getting married and naming our child Banafsaji, which is 'purple' in Arabic. Muslim summer-camp humour is very sophisticated.

Muslims can use any name as long as it doesn't have a negative connotation, such as 'piece of garbage'. As a result, Muslim names run the gamut. For some reason the name Natasha had really caught on among Pakistani Muslims. It means 'born on Christmas Day'. Some Muslims disapprove, though I heard one mother tell a critic that the real meaning was 'gift from God', which was a brilliant comeback.

I looked at my father. 'I wish you'd been able to stop her.'

My parents were living near Liverpool, and on the day I was born my father was on his way to his work as an engineer on the Mersey Tunnel. It was raining hard. He was stopped at a red light when a tractor-trailer slid across the intersection, lost control and hit him head-on.

My father's injuries were extensive. His knees and ribs were broken, and all the skin and muscle was torn off his forehead. Miraculously, his skull was not crushed. And horribly, extra-ordinarily, at that exact moment, halfway around the world, my mother's parents were on their way to a wedding close to Faisalabad when their car was also hit head-on by a truck. The groom, who was travelling with them, was killed instantly, as was my grandfather. My grandmother was critically injured and died a few days later.

My mother gave birth alone on 1 October 1967, in Liverpool University Hospital, unsure if her husband would survive his car accident, but unaware that her parents had not survived in Pakistan. No one would tell her the truth about her parents until they were sure my father would survive his injuries. In one fell swoop, my mother's life as a privileged, bourgeois daughter ended forever and she very nearly became a widow and a single mother too.

'I was dying in a hospital across town when your mother named you,' my father said.

'Let's not be so dramatic,' said my mother. 'You always told me I could choose the name.' And she had.

My brothers, Muzammal and Muddaththir, didn't escape the naming hell either. They were named after two chapters in the Qur'an. No one other than Muslims can pronounce either name properly. I was trying hard to avoid the fate all three of us had suffered. I wanted a name for my baby that was both pronounceable and meant something good.

I lay in bed at 6 a.m. staring at my bulbous belly, wondering if I had squandered the nine months by not thinking of a back-up name, and suddenly I felt the contractions. Sami insisted we go to the hospital. The contractions started five minutes apart, and within hours I was fully dilated.

'Could I have an epidural?' I begged.

'Too late,' said Dr McMaster.

'No,' I yelled, 'it's not too late!'

My doctor urged me to push. I bore down one more time and then, in what felt like passing a kidney stone the size of a turkey, a baby came out of me. I didn't even have a chance to see what had nearly torn out my innards because she was whisked away by a nurse for inspection.

'Now you just have to deliver the placenta,' said Dr McMaster matter-of-factly.

'Could I get an epidural first?' I asked.

Sami was overjoyed by the whole process.

'That was so easy,' he said as he stared in wonder at our new daughter.

Luckily for him, I couldn't reach the scalpels from where I lay shivering on my too-narrow table. Sami whispered the call to prayer in our daughter's tiny ear, as is the custom. And then I remembered she was still nameless.

'What's going to happen if we don't name her right away?' I asked Sami. 'Does the hospital name her?'

'I doubt it. I'm sure we have time.'

'Do you think it's wrong for Muslims to call their baby by the name Christian?'

'It might be confusing for some people,' replied Sami, as he swaddled our nameless newborn. 'Like an atheist naming their child Muhammad.'

With Maysa out of the running, I was still searching for my baby's perfect name.

'I think we should avoid names used by terrorists,' I told Sami.

'Yes, we won't name her Osama or Adolf, to be on the safe side,' he replied.

'We need a name,' I said anxiously.

'We have a name,' pointed out Sami.

But my mother's objection made me nervous, so I phoned my old Islamic-school teacher and asked if there was anything about the name Maysa that I should be aware of. He looked up a compendium of names of people who lived during the time of the Prophet.

'There was a Maysa who was a poet back then,' he said.

'What did she write about? Love?'

'Agriculture.'

'She never had her eyes plucked out, by chance?' It never hurts to ask.

'Not that I know of.'

I decided that my mother had had her chance at naming kids, and now it was mine.

'I'm naming her Maysa.'

'They'll call her Mess-up,' my mother said in her final attempt to dissuade me.

'That's better than what people called me,' I said, determined not to waver.

We took Maysa out for a walk in her pushchair and ran into a neighbour who had moved to Canada from Chile.

'What a beautiful baby,' she said. 'Can I hold her?'

Sami handed her over.

'She's got beautiful brown eyes,' said the neighbour. 'What's her name?'

'Maysa,' I said proudly.

'Ah,' said the neighbour frowning. 'That's an odd choice.'

'Why?' I asked, suddenly panicked. 'It doesn't mean "blue" in Spanish, does it?'

'No, *mesa* means "table".'

'It also means "gift from God",' I said as Sami eyed me.

The neighbour gave Maysa a quick kiss before handing her back.

'Sure it does,' she said.

I decided not to tell my mother.

Hajj

'Would you like to go for hajj?' asked my father-in-law.

'I really shouldn't. I'm trying to lose my baby weight. But maybe a tiny piece?'

'Not fudge, *hajj*,' he replied patiently. 'Would you like to go for hajj?'

Hajj and fudge have nothing to do with each other except that one is a religious requirement and the other I eat as if it *were* a religious requirement. And the words rhyme really well.

Go for hajj. The words pinged off each other in my brain.

All Muslims, once in their lives, are required to visit Mecca in Saudi Arabia, to perform the religious rituals there in the oldest mosque in the world, as an act of submission to God's will. It's one of the five pillars of Islam: going for hajj, belief in one God, praying the five daily prayers, fasting during the month of Ramadan, and giving 2.5 per cent of one's savings to charity. The hajj can occur only during Dhu al-Hijjah, the last month of the Islamic calendar.

Almost everyone goes. In the past, it was difficult for disabled Muslims to perform hajj, but through extensive renovations to facilities, the Saudis have made it possible for almost anyone to do it. Now, Muslims have developed a bad habit of waiting until they are old and decrepit before going – the last hurrah on the Muslim bucket list.

I dimly recalled that my parents had gone for hajj separately while I was a teenager. My father had gone first with relatives while my mother looked after us three kids, and the next year they switched. My life was currently consumed by a baby; the most important thing on my bucket list was to find time to take a nap. Sami and I married, set up house in Saskatchewan and had Maysa in just under a year. But I had finished a contract at the CBC and was unsure about which way my career was going. I was feeling a little unmoored. I could use a distraction. And a vacation. Suddenly hajj sounded perfect.

Then I started calculating how much it would cost to get from the Midwest to the Middle East.

'I'm paying for everyone,' said my father-in-law. That included Sabreena and Munir, Sami's brother and sister, and their spouses, Amir and Samira.

I agreed immediately.

'You know this isn't going to be like going to Club Med, right?' said Sami when he came home from work and found me sitting on the sofa, newspaper on my lap, dreaming.

He was ruining my reverie. Visions of a romantic holiday complete with sun and sand consumed me. I wondered if they had (non-alcoholic) drinks with little umbrellas in them.

Our apartment was an explosion of plastic neon-coloured

toys and stuffed animals. There were splats of tomato with dried-up spaghetti stuck on the walls. The source of those mealtime tantrums came tottering into the room clutching her favourite plush cat, which made purring sounds when you shook it. Maysa was twelve months old and was already speaking. She wandered over to me, flung her cat against the wall – producing a choked purr – pointed at my breasts, eyeing them covetously, and said, 'Yum.'

I shifted the newspaper to cover my chest. Love her as much as I did, I could really use a break from being a new mother.

I'd been breastfeeding her every two hours throughout the night since she was born. I had figured she would eventually outgrow her habit, but no, instead, like a crack addict she grew insatiable. My breasts were her dealers, doling out their contents every two hours, taking her to oblivion. If she didn't get what she wanted, she would scream and howl like a wounded animal until I finally relented. After a year of this, I was on the brink of a nervous breakdown from lack of sleep. Sami could see I was dying.

'End the night feeds,' he had insisted. 'After six months, babies are able to get through the night without food. We'll ferberize her.'*

The idea seemed sensible enough. We would go into her room at ever-increasing intervals to soothe her without feeding until she fell asleep on her own. But, like any addict worth her salt, she went down screaming.

'You're hurtin' me!' she'd yell as she pounded on her door at night. 'Somebody help me!' We'd been forced to move her

---

*Dr Richard Ferber wrote a famous book, *Solve Your Child's Sleep Problems*, in 1985 and his method is popularly referred to as 'ferberizing'.

to a futon on the floor after she had nearly fallen out of her cot in an attempt to find my breasts.

'We really should have started this before she could talk. What about the neighbours?' I said.

'We'll just have to explain to social services that we're sleep-training a child,' said Sami, calmly steering me away from the door.

After a few days, the screaming died down, and I began to remember what it was like to dream again. As I sat having dinner with George Clooney – 'Why yes, I *am* free to come to Lake Como for the weekend, but I might be going for hajj' – a tiny, furious raccoon attacked me.

George looked at me with shock in his eyes, and I startled out of my sleep to find Maysa on me. She had learned to turn the doorknob in her bedroom and escaped.

'Is this worth it?' I asked Sami as he snapped a white plastic cover on Maysa's doorknob the next morning.

'We should have done this when she was six months old,' said Sami. 'It would have been easier.'

'Do you think she'll be scarred for life?'

'She'll never remember.'

'I feel like a terrible parent,' I moaned.

'Do you ever want to sleep again?' said Sami. 'Because this could go on for years. And then *you'll* be scarred for life.'

'Make sure that doorknob protector is snapped on properly.'

After ten more days of screaming, Maysa finally gave up the fight. I could sleep. We had won the war.

The next morning, I started weaning her off breast milk during the day too.

I handed Maysa a sippy cup full of milk, which she flung

away in disdain. She stared at my breasts like a dog stares at a steak.

Strict parenting was no match for full-blown addiction. I needed to cut all ties with her dealer.

'Mama's breasts are going on vacation,' I said.

I sold my mother on the idea of taking Maysa for two weeks by telling her that she was now sleep-trained and totally weaned.

'This isn't work-related, is it?' asked my mother, suspicious.

'Nope, we're going for hajj.'

She couldn't believe her ears.

'Really, you?'

'Why is that so hard to believe?' I was actually a little insulted.

'Hajj is a spiritual journey. You have to be in the right frame of mind.'

'I can be spiritual,' I said, thinking about how to decide between an open-toed shoe and a sandal. Which would let in less sand?

Sami and I met my parents at the airport in Toronto on our stop-over from Regina. While we waited, Maysa pushed an empty luggage cart. I wasn't sure how to say goodbye. I knew she'd be upset if she saw me go.

'Just let her push the cart,' my father said as he lured her down the hallway by getting her to chase him. It worked like a charm. An Air Canada luggage cart had just replaced my breasts. I went through security and turned just in time to see the back of a tiny, happy girl who had no idea what was happening.

I felt guilty. I knew my parents would look after her every need. But what would go through her head when she finally got bored of the luggage cart? Would she think I had just abandoned her? Sami knew what I was thinking.

'She'll be fine,' he said. 'It's been a challenging year with her. You could use a break.' And then I walked down the hallway, feeling a sense of relief wash over me. I was no longer responsible for another human being's every physical and emotional need. I could finally concentrate on me.

'This is a big deal,' said Sami as I gleefully searched for the most adult movie on my little screen after take-off. No more singing monkeys dressed in overalls.

'I know,' I said, giddy with anticipation.

'What are you hoping for?'

'I hope *The Usual Suspects* is out on video by now,' I said, punching the buttons.

'Not entertainment-wise,' said Sami, irritated.

'Oh, umm, free almonds.'

'I meant hajj.'

I knew he wanted to hear something spiritual – something I was never good at expressing. 'To be a better Muslim. Connect with God, stuff like that' sounded like something I'd say to pacify my Islamic teacher at the mosque. But it still resonated, even if it was a close second to the almonds. And my vacation from being a mom. Even third place was good, right?

'What about you?' I asked.

'Free orange juice.'

'Very funny,' I said. 'Really, what are you hoping for?'

'I'm not sure. But it'll be nice to spend time as a couple.'

Darn it. I should have said that.

'It'll be our official honeymoon,' I said, taking his hand.

'Did you read the hajj handbook?' He let go of my hand and put a small booklet in my palm. So unromantic.

I looked in the handbook. I knew a little bit about hajj already.

Visiting the Kaaba in the city of Mecca was a big deal, but the booklet described a myriad places and things and prayers. My fondness for religious rules and regulations had waned since I was a teenager. I wanted faith to be simpler and less cluttered.

The flight attendant came by with the dinner selection.

'This is complicated,' I said. 'There are so many things here.'

'Don't worry, hajj gets easier once you're on the ground and can see what all the procedures are,' said Sami. Then he saw me staring at the menu. 'You're just talking about the food selection, aren't you?'

'No, I'm reading the manual.' I forced my eyes back to the byzantine world of the hajj manual.

'The manual is important because hajj gets overwhelming with the sheer number of people. It's important to know what's happening so we'll be safe. I know because I did it as a teenager.' I pictured him in a cape and tights with a capital S on his chest, for 'Superhajji'. I stifled a laugh.

'Yeah, there's really useful information in this,' I said.

'Like what?'

'Like apparently the malls are incredible.'

We landed at Jeddah Airport with hundreds of other exhausted but excited people. All of us had to put on clothing referred to as *ihram*, which was all we would wear for the duration of hajj. Sami, along with all the men, put on two sheets of unstitched white fabric, the size of large bath towels, which is the male hajj uniform. One sheet went around his waist and the other draped over one of his shoulders.

Dressing identically eliminates any signs of wealth or status: kings and paupers look the same. Basically, hajj looks like the world's biggest toga party, with less emphasis on the party. Women wear stitched but simple clothes, including modest underwear. Face coverings, such as the niqab, are not allowed during hajj. I was wearing a grey cotton shalwar kameez and white cotton headscarf.

Even though it was only May, it was stiflingly hot. People were walking with prayer beads in their hands, reciting prayers. Just making it this far felt like a huge accomplishment. I noticed that almost everyone had a booklet in their own language explaining the rituals of hajj. It was like we were all taking the same exam. The airport officials ushered each planeload of people into the immigration and customs section of the terminal quickly and efficiently. They couldn't afford delays, since hundreds of planes from around the world were coming in continuously. Hajj is one of the biggest human pilgrimages in the world. Mecca, a city with a resident population of two million, swells to twice or three times that size during hajj.

Our passports and papers were examined and we were given wristbands, the kind you get when you enter amusement parks to prove you've paid your entry fee. There was Arabic writing on them.

'What's this?' I asked Sami, who said this was different from when he went to hajj as a teenager in the 1970s. He checked the manual and then told me that with ever-increasing numbers of people coming to Mecca every year from all over the world, speaking different languages, the Saudis now tagged everyone. In case anyone got separated from his or her group, there was a human lost-and-found section based on country of origin.

The Saudis faced a logistical nightmare keeping pilgrims sorted, fed, hydrated and alive. Every year pilgrims die from accidents, old age and epidemics. There was a dedicated morgue with coolers for hundreds of dead people, and a cemetery, Jannat al Baqi, out back. You die at hajj, you get buried at hajj. But Muslims consider it a blessing to be buried in the same cemetery as the companions and relatives of the Prophet. It was an open secret that some people waited to do the hajj until they were old in the hope of being buried there. It must be a bitter disappointment to them to go home alive.

Going through security was quick. Serious-looking men rifled through our suitcases. My *Vanity Fair* was confiscated. I looked at Sami.

'I told you to read the manual,' he said unsympathetically. 'It tells you they're big on censorship.'

I didn't have time to sulk because we were immediately loaded on to a bus that took us on the hour-long journey to Mecca. We travelled on a four-lane highway through the desert, which was dotted with small hills and shrubbery. The passengers on the bus started the Talbiyah chant, the official hajj prayer – *Labbaykah-allahumma labbaykah*, which means 'Here I am, O Allah, here I am. Here I am, you have no partner, here I am. Indeed all praise, grace and sovereignty belong to you.' It was hypnotic listening to everyone repeat the same melodic prayer as we swayed together on the bus. The growing anticipation was a charge in the air.

When we got to our air-conditioned, five-star hotel in Mecca, I lay on the crisp bed and luxuriated in the fine linen. My first hajj, and I loved it.

'We should do this every year,' I told Sami as I made a snow angel on the fluffy down duvet.

He lay down on the bed beside me.

'Mmm–hmm,' I said, nuzzling up to him. 'We don't have to worry about a little tiny creature disturbing us.'

'No,' he said playfully. 'But just tell me one thing.'

'Sure.'

'Did you read the manual?'

'Of course,' I lied as I snuggled closer.

'So you know sex is forbidden during the hajj.'

'WHAT?' I nearly choked. 'Why would God do that?'

'Probably because God knew that *some people* wouldn't focus on anything else.'

'Really, no sex during the whole thing?'

'There might be a window of opportunity between umrah and hajj,' he said, laughing. 'But you'll have to read the handbook to be sure.'

This time I grabbed the handbook with real appreciation. The hajj consists of two sections. The *umrah* is a preamble, a lesser hajj to be done first, and involves two main rituals: *tawaf*, circling the Kaaba seven times in a counter-clockwise direction, and *sa'i*, walking between the two hills of Safa and Marwah. Then the clothing for hajj, the ihram, is removed, and people take a break and engage in activities that normally aren't allowed, like sex, until the eighth day of Dhu al-Hijjah, at which point the official hajj begins. All the pilgrims, now wearing ihram again, travel to the tent city of Mina, visit the neighbouring areas of Muzdalifah and Arafat, and perform *ramy*, the symbolic stoning of the Devil. Then, back in Mecca, men shave their heads while women remove about a centimetre of hair, and an animal is sacrificed to commemorate Eid al-Adha. Adha is the day the Prophet Abraham sacrificed an animal in place of his son.

Then finally another tawaf and sa'i, after which the ihram

can be taken off, marking the end of hajj, and all the restrictions, including that on sex, are lifted. I was out of luck for the next four to five days, but I could see at least the hajj would keep me busy.

Sabreena, Sami's sister, knocked on our door.

'Did I get you at a bad time?'

'Unfortunately, no,' I said.

'Do you want to come with me to circle the Kaaba?' she asked.

'Sure.' I picked out my best sandals for the visit.

'I should come with you,' said Sami. 'It gets pretty crowded. Did you read the section on—'

'We'll be fine,' I said breezily as I took Sabreena's arm. I was tired of hajj being theoretical. I wanted to do the real thing.

As we walked out of the hotel and turned a corner, the Kaaba, the box-like structure at the centre of the mosque, suddenly appeared in front of us. I stopped breathing for a second. I'd seen pictures in books since I was old enough to know I was Muslim, but to actually see it, in the brick, was something else. I was surprised by how emotional I felt. The central tenet of Islam is to believe in an unseen and unrepresented god. Our entire lives, we pray towards the direction of the Kaaba. *Kaaba* literally means 'cube' in Arabic, and now here it was: a simple structure enshrouded in black silk cloth with verses of the Qur'an embroidered in gold near the top. I felt my throat constrict as I looked at the building, and felt a powerful connection to the past. Muslims believe Abraham and his son Ismail built the original structure as a house of worship, but I had to remind myself that it had been completely rebuilt over the centuries and this particular structure wasn't from ancient times.

I stood there, staring at this symbol of my faith, and a verse in the Qur'an – 'They will come to thee on foot and on every kind of fast mount, coming from every faraway point on earth' – rang through my head and reminded me of the quote from *Field of Dreams*: 'If you build it, they will come.' And they had come. A sea of humanity was circling the Kaaba in a counter-clockwise direction. As Sabreena and I got near, the noise became deafening. From far away, the movement had looked peaceful and orderly, but as we got closer we noticed a lot of pushing and shoving. Patience is a prerequisite of hajj, but it was easy to see how people could become agitated. Most of the frenzy was in the rows of people closest to the Kaaba, where people wanted to touch the Kaaba and were moving in closer. Their real goal was the black stone, the *Mona Lisa* of the Muslim world, which is encased in an oval silver structure and used to count the rotations of the tawaf. Although touching the black stone is not a required part of hajj, because the Prophet had kissed it during hajj people were becoming emotional and kept trying to stop and kiss it.

'It feels so sacred,' I said as I watched the whole mess of chanting pilgrims moving around the Kaaba. When I finally managed to tear my eyes away and look around me, I saw a McDonald's, a KFC and a Rolex store. The Saudis have a strange way of preserving the past. Ancient Muslim sites, such as mosques, tombs and homes of the early historical figures of Islam, have been replaced by luxury hotels and malls. The official justification is that Muslims would worship the sites themselves and not God, so they had to go. There's been an outcry in the Muslim world at the loss of its collective heritage under Saudi control. The Saudis follow an extremely austere form of religion, called Wahhabism or

Salafism, and unilaterally enforce anything they deem un-
Islamic.

'It's like we went to Vegas and hajj broke out,' I said to
Sabreena, a little dismayed by the large, opulent structures
surrounding us.

The ground around the Kaaba is covered with marble to
keep it from eroding under the constant movement of foot-
steps. We left our sandals by the entrance to the building that
contains the Kaaba and joined the surge of people orbiting
it. It felt like getting sucked into an eddy of humans, and it
was oddly beautiful. We were with thousands of people who
shared our faith, moving in unison in an act of pilgrimage.
Old people lying on stretchers were carried by burly attendants. Toddlers bobbed above the crowd on the shoulders of
their fathers. We were all doing what our ancestors had done
for thousands of years. Sabreena and I got so caught up in the
moment that we were swept away, and suddenly we found
ourselves too close to the Kaaba, where the crowd became
unbearably dense. I linked arms with Sabreena so we
wouldn't get separated. As we neared the black stone, people
stopped to pray and the people behind kept pressing. I was
being squeezed until I couldn't breathe. My ribs started to
bend painfully, but I couldn't even fall down because I was so
compressed. Panic and fear overwhelmed me. I lost Sabreena.
There was simply no way to escape the crowd. At the
moment I felt I was going to black out from the pain, the
crowd eased again and Sabreena was suddenly beside me.

'That was horrible,' I said, breathing deeply, relieved it was
over. And then someone grabbed my breast and squeezed it.
'Sabreena!' I yelled. 'Someone's touching me.'

I could only get a vague sense of a figure beside me, and
then he disappeared into the crowd. We looked around but

there was no way to find the culprit. We worked our way out of the crowd as fast as possible. I was so shocked I couldn't speak at first. All the holiness went out of hajj like a deflated balloon. That was the last thing on earth I thought would happen in a place like this. The intimacy of being surrounded by all these Muslims, which had made me feel so warm and cherished moments before, was now gone. In front of Islam's holiest symbol, there were perverts circling around hoping to cop a feel. I felt violated and furious at the person who did this, and I wanted him to be punished. But there was no finding him in that lava flow of people.

'What just happened?' I asked.

'I think you just got sexually assaulted in front of the Kaaba,' said Sabreena.

'What's wrong?' Sami asked as soon as he saw me coming through the door of our hotel room.

Sami held me as I explained what had happened. I had wanted so badly to get away, to have a break from Maysa, but now I all wanted was to be home with my little girl. And I felt she would be just as appalled as I was, given her affinity for my breasts.

'Don't ever go there alone again,' he said.

'That shouldn't happen here,' I said. 'The Kaaba should be the safest place on earth.'

'Muslims are just people, and people do bad things.'

'What happened to hajj being an experience of spiritual enlightenment? It says here, in the manual, everyone has to focus on their relationship with God. No gossiping, no rudeness, no swearing.' I flapped the booklet. 'It doesn't actually say no groping, but I think that's implied!'

'Look, not everyone here is here for the hajj. It's like anywhere that draws large numbers of people – you're going to have some people who come to take advantage.'

I couldn't believe how naïve I had been. I lay down on the bed, trying to calm down. 'And someone stole my sandals.'

'It did say in the manual to wear a cheap pair of sandals so no one would be tempted to steal them,' said Sami.

'Can't I just feel sorry for myself?' I said, annoyed by his practicality.

Sami and I sat quietly together for a while.

Finally he spoke. 'What can I do to make hajj better for you?'

'I just want to hate this person and not be judged for it.'

'Fine. And we're going together on the rest of the rituals,' he said as he tightened his ihram.

'You're not wearing underwear, are you?'

'No,' said Sami, looking a little vulnerable. Underwear is a stitched garment and therefore is forbidden for men.

'You better hope there aren't any female gropers in that crowd,' I said.

On our way to the Kaaba the call for evening prayer started, erupting out of loudspeakers set up throughout the city. I've always loved the sound of the *azan*; melodic and serene and so familiar. It was comforting to hear the same words that I was used to hearing back home. The echoing, tinny loudspeaker voice soothed me. Everyone just stopped in their tracks and lined up for prayer. The crowd around the Kaaba stood for prayers, radiating outwards into all the streets and sidewalks of the surrounding areas, all space filled with people. Men and women stood side by side. This was new for me. Muslims are normally manic about separating women from men, with women taking the subordinate positions in mosques, but here in Mecca, the genders are ordered to pray together in mixed lines. Because the Prophet did not leave instructions to alter this arrangement, it's never been allowed to change. I could tell the men weren't happy praying next to me, but they had no choice.

'I wish we could pray like this all the time,' I said to Sami.

Sami was well versed in my rage about the separation of men and women's prayer spaces. In many mosques I've attended, women have to pray behind some sort of partition, like a curtain. Praying in this sea of men and women together, as they had been doing for fourteen hundred years, felt like a hopeful sign that change was possible in the mosques around the world.

When the prayers were over, Sami and I walked to the Kaaba, but this time we kept to the outer circle of pilgrims where there was more space. We noticed that male members of families formed a circle around their female relatives to keep them safe. I should have been more observant and less idealistic when I was with Sabreena. This time I was able to finish all seven circumambulations of tawaf without incident. Afterwards we said our prayers in a more isolated corner of the enclosed gated area, to avoid being trampled.

The next day we joined the rest of Sami's family for the ritual of sa'i. Muslims believe that Abraham was ordered by God to take his wife, Hajar, and infant son, Ismail, to an uncultivated valley in the desert. He gave her some water and dates and started to leave them. A confused Hajar asked Abraham if this was what God had ordered him to do, and he said yes. She said, 'We are not going to be lost, since God, who has commanded you, is with us.' She waited under the hot sun, but after she ran out of food and water she started to become frantic and ran between two hills, Safa and Marwah, looking for help. After her seventh run, Ismail kicked the sand and water began to gush out. A caravan of travellers came and asked permission to share the water. Gradually people settled in that area, which became known as Mecca, and built a well, which is known as Zam Zam, one of the oldest wells in history.

The ritual today no longer resembles a desperate run between two sandy hills. Now it's like walking in a giant air-conditioned convention centre, with marble walls and floors and an ornate ceiling with chandeliers and fans overhead. There are even water stations to slake your thirst. Hajar would have appreciated that.

There are three walking lanes separated from each other by columns. The right lane is for people moving from Safa to Marwah, a distance of 450 metres. The left lane is for people going in the opposite direction; and the middle lane is reserved for people pushing wheelchairs. As we entered the tunnel, we noticed the one nod to what the journey had once been – a piece of exposed rock at the end of the lanes, representing the original hills, which have now been mostly worn away. People sat on the polished rock reciting prayers.

'It's illegal to export Zam Zam water,' Sami told me as we stopped for a drink of the water. I felt like the world's slowest, holiest marathoner with my tiny paper cup.

'Why?' I asked. He loves knowing this stuff, so I try to humour him.

'Because of its religious significance, people try to bottle it for sale. So Saudi Arabia banned its export and gives it away to pilgrims for free. But people still bottle regular tap water and try to pass it off as Zam Zam water.'

'People can be horrible.' I sat on the stones to rest my feet.

'How are you feeling about things?' asked Sami.

'I feel better,' I said, sipping my water. This part of our trip hadn't been crowded. The Saudis had made sure there was enough room to accommodate people. To me, the journey was symbolic of a woman's faith in the face of terrible circumstances. Hajar had obviously been scared and worried about her baby, but she never lost hope. Several thousand years later we remember her resilience. Saudi Arabia doesn't let women travel without permission from a man, and yet here were millions of Muslims retracing the steps of Hajar, a woman who had been left alone in the desert with no resources. She could have been attacked, and yet she had been safer than even me, who lived in modern times.

'I would have made a pathetic Hajar,' I told Sami. 'I would have just followed Abraham back to safety.'

'I'm sure God would have made a mirage in the desert to keep your hopes alive,' said Sami, smiling.

'Of what?'

'A barista.'

Afterwards, we decided to visit the myriad bazaars that line the city.

'Wow, this place is a Mecca for shoppers,' I said.

Sami looked at me.

'Sorry, too easy.'

We saw a group of people milling around an escalator, pointing and gesturing to each other. My heart stopped. I thought there had been an accident. But as we got closer, we realized that the draw was the escalator itself. In my life of privilege, it never occurred to me that there would be people here who came from remote areas of the world and had never been to a three-storey shopping mall with escalators. Oddly, I felt as humbled by the escalator as by the Kaaba. If Muslims weren't ordered to perform hajj, these people might never have had a chance to travel. Sami and I stopped for a moment to watch the pilgrims as they urged each other to try the escalator.

Everyone, poor or rich, wanted to take advantage of the extraordinary shopping opportunities. I was looking at a toy cellphone for Maysa at a makeshift stall when a young Bangladeshi vendor came up to me.

'Do you speak English?' he asked.

'Yes, why?'

'My fiancée sent me this letter and I can't read English well. Could you translate it for me?'

I looked at the letter: *I want you to mail me new videos of the latest movies. I didn't like the ones you sent last week.*

'I'm not sure this is the woman for you,' I said to the vendor.

Sami whispered in my ear, 'It's not your business to comment on his love life.'

'How could she not like *Pulp Fiction* and *Shawshank*?' I whispered back. 'She's got terrible taste.'

'You didn't like *Star Trek II, The Wrath of Khan*,' Sami hissed. 'And I still married you.'

'Did she get the videos I sent her?' asked the vendor anxiously.

'Yes, she did, and here's the list of what she wants now.' I pointed the items out for him. 'Send her *Ace Ventura: Pet Detective*. Given her tastes, she'll probably like that one.'

The vendor thanked us profusely and pushed two rolled-up plastic mats into our hands.

'What are these?' I asked Sami.

'They're hajji mats, I think. We'll use them in Mina,' he said. 'Let's find you a good but ugly pair of sandals. Tomorrow's going to be tough.'

Once we'd found me some new footwear, I whined until

Sami agreed to let me buy a kebab. Sami's father had adamantly warned us against eating food from street vendors, but what he didn't know wouldn't hurt him. As I chewed away happily, we stumbled upon Sami's parents buying some prayer mats to take home. I quickly hid the kebab wrapping. God was giving me a rough time. We exchanged stories about our day, then agreed to meet early the next morning.

'Make sure you pack light tomorrow,' said Sami's father. 'We have a long journey ahead of us.'

The next day we got on a bus heading for the tent city of Mina. Mina is significant because it's where Abraham was ordered by God to sacrifice his son. The Devil then came and tried to dissuade Abraham from fulfilling his duty. The road was clogged with thousands of buses, inching along in a swirl of smog and pollution. The valley of Mina is only five kilometres east of Mecca, but because of the traffic, it took us three hours to get there. The journey was a huge test of patience, as if traffic jams and the Devil were linked some-how. But even the Devil couldn't keep the hordes of Muslims from eventually reaching Mina.

The Saudis had built a temporary tent city to accommo-date the millions of pilgrims. As far as I could look was a sea of identical white tents. Sections of the valley were divided into different continents and then subdivided into different countries, so in theory pilgrims could find their area more easily. It took us several hours to find North America, and then Canada. The Canadian 'tent' was four poles and a white awning: no walls, no floor. I looked at the dirt and rocks on the ground.

'Are you sure there aren't any hotels nearby?' I asked.

'No hotels allowed. We're just going to be camping out for

the next few days,' said Sami. 'And we're fortunate that your friend gave us these.' He laid out the two hajji mats.

I was speechless. Now I knew I should have read the manual. I'd been camping, but this was more austere. By now it was night – not that it was any cooler – and we said our prayers and got ready to sleep. We lay down on our hajji mats, which were thinner than I'd realized – I could feel all the rocks and pebbles beneath me. The Hilton this wasn't. I curled up next to Sami.

'Now it makes sense why sex isn't allowed during hajj,' I said as we tried to get comfortable. 'This place could erupt into a giant orgy. The Saudis, despite their billions, would never be able to police us all.'

'It's good you think of these things at the right moments,' he said, trying to sleep.

In the morning, after prayers, Sabreena and I headed off in search of food. The tent city was like a real city, with mini-markets that sold pilgrim essentials. As we made our way through it, I quickly realized that when you're sleeping among lots of strange men who aren't wearing underwear, you have to be careful where you look.

While we prudently picked our way around the modestly compromised, I felt spasms in my stomach. I knew this feeling: I needed to find a bathroom. Fast.

'You didn't eat any of the food from the stalls, did you?' asked Sabreena.

'Maybe just a little,' I said sheepishly.

Since the Saudis had to house millions of us, they also had to deal with our toilet needs. Sabreena and I went to the rows and rows of cubicles. The floor of each cubicle was lined with white plastic that extended into a neat hole in the middle. There was a hose attached to the wall of the cubicle.

Many pilgrims came from countries and cultures where an above-ground toilet is not common, and plunging a toilet isn't an option in the desert. But I had never used a squat toilet before. Sabreena looked at me.

'They're not hard to use,' she said. 'Just don't fall in.'

My stomach gurgled. I went in and was surprised by how much it didn't smell. I used the hose to wash the white plastic floor to make myself feel better about hygiene. Then I made sure the door was locked, took off my clothes and put them in a corner because I didn't want anything to get dirty. I wouldn't be changing clothes for the next three days.

When Sabreena and I returned to the tent thirty minutes later, with no food in hand and me looking a little ashen, Sami's dad gave me a knowing look. I nodded meekly.

'Try to eat as little as you can,' he said.

'I know,' I said. 'Less ammo for my stomach.'

I strenuously avoided eating and just drank water, which evaporated as sweat so quickly that I didn't need to use the plastic cubicle. There were hawkers selling umbrellas, and Sami's father bought one for each of us. It wasn't rain that people were worried about. The tiny bit of shade the umbrella provided while walking around the camp was a mercy. We were supposed to spend our downtime in prayer and reflection. I lay down on the ground, feeling very grateful for the highlights of my world at this point: the tents and the toilets.

The next day we left by creaky, un-air-conditioned bus for what pilgrims call the heart of the hajj – the plain of Arafat, which is a stretch of desert where the Prophet gave his last hajj sermon, 'the Farewell Sermon'. It was a fourteen-kilometre journey.

School buses drove by with open tops that looked as if someone had taken a can opener and removed the roof.

'Did you see that?' I asked Sami.

'Some Shia sects discourage the use of any shelter during hajj. They're trying to be authentic to the real experience.'

'I couldn't deal with that in this heat,' I said.

And then suddenly I had to.

Our bus made a terrible squealing sound, and stopped. It had overheated.

The driver wanted us to walk the rest of the way. It was already stiflingly hot on the bus, but when we got off, it felt like stepping into an oven. It was 120 degrees (48°C). I watched the roofless bus pass us by and I was jealous. Up to that point we had done our rituals at night to avoid the punishing heat, but there was no getting away from it now. The umbrellas provided some relief, but what really helped me was pouring a whole bottle of water on my head.

'What are you doing?' asked Sami.

'This actually cools you off for about fifteen minutes, but then you get dry again. If it wasn't so horrible, it would be amazing.' I dumped another bottle of water on my head. Luckily for us, the Saudis made water available in refrigerated lorries that were parked along the route, in order to reduce the number of pilgrims who die of dehydration every year. I noticed some pilgrims pulling a suitcase. They looked exhausted. I was glad I had heeded my father-in-law's advice and brought only a small backpack.

At the plains of Arafat, people read the Farewell Sermon. As they read, 'All mankind is from Adam and Eve, an Arab has no superiority over a non-Arab nor a non-Arab has any superiority over an Arab; also a white has no superiority over black nor a black has any superiority over white except by piety and good action,' I remembered reading *Snow White and the Seven Dwarves* to Maysa but changing the words to 'Potato Head and the Seven Dwarves' so she wouldn't get a complex, which was ironic since she had inherited her father's fair skin. As a child, I knew that fair skin was coveted in our community and wondered if my brown skin meant I wasn't pretty. These words from 1,400 years ago still resonated for me.

That evening we left for Muzdalifah, another rocky valley, by bus. At Muzdalifah, the plan was that we would collect rocks for the next day's ritual, then combine Maghrib and Isha, the last two prayers of the day, before settling in for the night. But there were no tents.

'So where do we sleep?' I asked.

'Just on the ground,' said Sami. And just like that, after performing prayers and reading the Qur'an, people simply lay on the bare ground and slept. I couldn't sleep. I was feeling unwell. I could control my food poisoning if I stopped eating, but there were still painful spasms in my stomach. I noticed Sabreena was awake too.

'Can't sleep?' I asked her.

'There's a truck behind me that keeps spurting diesel.'

We both got up and looked around. It was eerie.

'This is supposed to remind us of death,' said Sabreena. 'We die naked and alone in the end. All we leave is our actions.'

Millions of people lay on the ground all around us in white clothing that now looked liked shrouds. I felt a chill go up my spine. It didn't matter how rich any of us were back home: we were all in the same boat, or rather, the same desert.

'It's like the end of days here,' I said. 'I wonder if it's going to look like this on the Day of Judgement, minus the trucks and the half-naked men.'

I saw a child nearby watching me as her mother read from the Qur'an. She was almost the same age as Maysa. She put her arms out and I looked at her mother, who nodded. I picked up the little girl and held her close. I missed that feeling. I missed Maysa. When the girl became agitated and wanted her own mother, I reluctantly gave her back.

I imagined what it must have been like for Abraham to be ordered to sacrifice his son. He had almost lost his son before, when he left Hajar alone in the desert, and then when God asked him to sacrifice Ishmael, he came so close again.* Abraham stopped three times because it's said the Devil tried to stop him. I imagine any parent would have had a difficult time. I wondered if Hajar's faith ever wavered, being left alone in the desert. At her most desperate hour, did she ever wonder if God had abandoned her?

Why did God want us to remember these painful stories? I could think of only one reason. Having faith is more than just believing; it's about living with fear and self-doubt and working through those feelings until they bring some sort of answer.

People started waking up for the pre-dawn prayers, and our valley of death turned into a valley of zombies as people lurched towards the cubicles to make their ablutions.

Sami woke up and looked at me.

'What are you doing?' he asked.

'Deciding what to do next with my life,' I answered.

'Should I be worried?'

---

*In the Christian tradition, Abraham was commanded to sacrifice Isaac.

'Let's have another baby.'

He looked surprised. 'Are you sure? Because it seems like you're pretty busy already.'

'And I'm going to leave journalism and try to make films instead,' I added. The feeling that journalism wasn't enough any more had been gnawing at me before I left. I wanted to tell stories. Maybe the ones I was reliving here inspired me. Hajj seemed to make the impossible possible, as I felt a sense of calm about decisions that had seemed agonizing at home. The cacophony of noise, people and physical suffering suddenly fell away and I was left with a feeling of conviction.

'Those are pretty big steps,' said Sami. 'Having a baby and changing careers.'

'I guess faith is about overcoming hardship and not being consumed by it,' I said, thinking about Hajar and Abraham again.

'Anything else?'

'I also thought that you make a good-looking corpse.'

We boarded our bus again and headed for a part of the valley named Ramy al-Jamaraat, where pilgrims gather small stones, no larger than a chickpea, and throw them at three pillars that are symbols for Satan.

As we approached the pillars I could hear a roar from the pilgrims closest to them. People were getting very emotional. Instead of pebbles, I could see flip-flops, water bottles and large rocks flying, alongside curses aimed at the Devil. Often the objects would miss the pillar and hit the pilgrims on the other side. It seemed like many people were getting carried away and had forgotten that this wasn't *actually* the Devil cast in modern-day concrete.

I knew that this was the most dangerous part of the hajj.

The previous year, 240 people had been crushed to death during stampedes. I felt a wave of panic as the crowds became more dense and agitated. My stomach heaved again from the food poisoning. I didn't have the physical stamina to enter this mob of agitated people.

'I can't do this,' I told Sami as memories of the crushing crowds around the Kaaba came back to me.

'It's OK,' he said. 'This looks too dangerous. We'll do it for you guys.'

Sami, Amir, Munir and my father-in-law continued on while the rest of us moved to safety. The four men disappeared into an angry vortex of people. I'd never thought I'd actually worry about Sami being crushed to death in a stampede of people out to stone the Devil.

'They'll be fine, *inshallah*,' said my mother-in-law as she noticed the three of us looking anxious. She was suffering from uncontrollable fits of coughing caused by the pollution and exhaustion. If anyone had a reason to complain about health problems it was her, but she was our pillar of strength. As I counted the minutes and listened to the deafening roar of furious pilgrims, I felt that I would be grateful to have my life back, screaming baby and all.

The men appeared suddenly by our sides.

'How was it?' I asked as I hugged Sami, so happy to see him in one piece.

'That was insane.' He described riled-up pilgrims yelling at the Devil about all the things they blamed him for: a bad boss, arthritis, a nagging mother-in-law. It would have been funny if it weren't so dangerous.

We headed back to Mecca, where we would perform tawaf and sa'i again. Sami went to have his head shaved, and I had a fingertip-width of hair cut from my head.

'Oh well,' said Sabreena when the men came back looking like shorn sheep. 'You have to let go of your pride.'

I ran my hand over Sami's head, which looked enormous without his beloved hair. 'Your head looks like a giant melon.'

'Thanks,' said Sami.

That just left the animal sacrifice. The Saudis had set up a system whereby we could purchase tickets to have a goat or sheep sacrificed on our behalf. The meat would be distributed to the poor. We didn't see any blood, and were grateful to just take the Saudis at their word when they said that everything was taken care of.

The major rites of hajj being finished, we were now able to remove our ihram.

We went back to our hotel and took hot showers, which seemed like heaven. As the water washed away the dirt and grime from days of travel in smog and desert, I felt happy and deeply satisfied. Hajj had been an emotionally and physically exhausting ordeal. I felt like I had accomplished something significant in my life.

When we arrived back in Toronto, my mother was holding Maysa, who looked much plumper than when we had left. She saw me, started to cry, jumped out of my mother's arms and ran to me.

'Every time she asked for you, I'd tell her you were in a plane,' said my mother. 'She spent the last two weeks staring at the sky as planes flew by and saying, "Pane, pane, Mama pane." I had to feed her constantly to keep her distracted.

'You did remember to pray for the salvation of your soul?' she asked.

'Of course.' I decided this wasn't the time to tell her I'd also prayed for my film career to prosper.

Sami took Maysa from me. 'Is she heavier?'

'Yeah, she just ate and stared at planes while we were gone,' I said. 'It will be amazing to have another baby.'

'After everything you've gone through with her, are you sure you want to start all over again?'

'Hey, I got groped and crushed, suffered from heatstroke, starvation, dehydration, food poisoning and insomnia, and I probably have black lung.'

'So having a baby doesn't seem so bad,' said Sami.

I hugged my father-in-law and thanked him for the opportunity to do hajj earlier than I had expected. He was pushing my mother-in-law in a wheelchair because she was too weak from her journey to walk.

'Did you get what you wanted out of hajj?' I asked him.

'I got to be with my family before all of you get too busy with your families.' He put something in my hand and headed for our connecting flight.

'What's that?' asked Sami.

I looked inside the paper bag.

It was a piece of fudge.

BBQ Muslims

'Is this Zarqa Nawaz?' asked an annoyed man when I picked up the phone.

'This is her.' I cradled the handset under my right ear while settling one-month-old Inaya to breastfeed. Inaya means 'gentle person', and other than a penchant for projectile vomiting, she had lived up to her name. Some babies are fussy eaters, but Inaya would latch on with the strength of a lamprey, which let me talk on the phone while blending chicken pieces to make toddler food for the fussy eater.

'I'm hungry!' yelled Maysa. I threw a bib on her as she climbed into her high chair.

'My name is Mario, and I'm calling from the Toronto International Film Festival. *BBQ Muslims* has been officially selected to participate in this year's festival. Congratulations,' he said. My finger paused on the pulse button.

After hajj I had taken a break from journalism and turned to filmmaking. To be sure I wasn't making a mistake, I took a summer film workshop at the Ontario College of Art as soon as I got back and submitted my student project to the Toronto International Film Festival. I figured if I got in, it would be a sign.

I dumped some blended chicken curry into a bowl, to the percussion of tiny fists pounding on the high-chair tray. 'I'm hungry!' Maysa repeated as she greedily grabbed the bowl.

I heard an exasperated sigh on the other end of the phone.

'What's wrong?' I asked.

'You *do* realize that thousands of people apply for this coveted spot? This is an incredible honour.'

'I'm really honoured. Really, I am,' I said, feeling guilty as I spooned chicken curry into Maysa's mouth and moved Inaya to the other breast.

'You forgot to put your address and phone number on the application form,' he fumed. Oh.

'How'd you find me?' I asked, amazed.

'I phoned every Nawaz in the greater Toronto area and finally found your brother in Burlington. He gave me your number.'

'It's a good thing I kept my maiden name.'

Maysa spat out her food. 'I worked hard making that.'

'You could have fooled me,' said Mario.

'Really, I blend curried chicken with lentils. It's the only thing she'll eat,' I said, indignant. 'Oh! I forgot to add the lentils.'

'I was talking about your film.'

I paused as I dumped both curries back into the blender. 'Wait, you're saying my film is . . . bad?'

'Those are not my exact words,' said Mario.

'So what did you mean by "You could have fooled me"?'

There was a three-second pause. Enough time to add some butter to my concoction and absorb what he had just said.

'There are filmmakers out there,' he finally said, 'who are going to say, "My technically perfect film was rejected for this."'

I felt my face flush. I was officially offended.

'What do you mean by "this"?' I said. Inaya detached herself from my breast, drunk with milk.

'It wasn't exactly professional, was it?'

'It was a student project,' I said, feeling a little defensive.

'Let me rephrase then. There are students out there who are going to be upset that their technically perfect film was rejected so your film could be accepted.'

'So why did you accept it?' I started to burp Inaya, who promptly vomited a geyser of milk on to me.

'Because we've never had a submission that dealt with your . . . topic before. We judged it on originality, not technicality. Despite its . . . shortcomings, it seemed to resonate at a certain level.'

I tried not to take the criticism personally. It had been a shotgun film.

'Think of a simple subject where you can make a quick five-minute film,' Terry, our instructor at the Ontario College of Art, had told us. 'Remember, you're not making a feature. You have to be able to finish it in one afternoon. You have forty-eight hours to come up with a concept, write it and pull everything together before you start shooting.'

I was feeding Maysa her breakfast at my mother's house, where I was staying during the course. As I looked at that morning's *Toronto Star*, I noticed a row of black and white photographs: Muslim suspects who had been arrested for the bombing of the Alfred P. Murrah Federal Building in Oklahoma City.

'Why would Muslims do such a horrible thing?' I wondered as I undid Maysa's high-chair and let her out. She toddled towards my mother. 'Innocent children died in that attack.'

'We don't know the whole story yet,' she said, pulling Maysa on to her lap. 'You become despondent so quickly.'

'They wouldn't be pulling Muslim suspects off planes if there wasn't any evidence,' I replied. 'They must know something.'

'Give people a chance,' said my mother, knowing I was sceptical of her good will.

The next day they arrested the very un-Muslim Timothy McVeigh.

'See?' said my mother.

'This makes no sense,' I replied. 'Why did they arrest people who bear no resemblance to the person who actually did it?'

'Perception can be a powerful thing,' she said.

I had found the perfect subject for my short film. Muslims certainly aren't completely innocent of all wrongdoing, but what happens when we are? I was going to examine how strongly held stereotypes can colour people's attitudes. I quickly wrote a script about two Muslim brothers who are asleep when a bomb explodes in their back yard. The neighbours turn against them and accuse the brothers of being Middle Eastern terrorists, even though they've never been to the Middle East. Despite their innocence, they're thrown into jail and left there. The real terrorists are two men from the Barbecue Anti-Resistance Front – BARF for short. The guys from BARF go around blowing up barbecues to bring attention to the cause of pollution in the environment and cannot believe their bad luck: having chosen a BBQ owned by Muslims, they can't get any attention.

'Are you going to hire actors for the film?' asked my mother.

'There's no budget. I'll just get volunteers. It's how Steven Spielberg started.'

'I don't think it's that easy to find people,' she said.

'You'd be surprised at how many people secretly want to act.'

'Use relatives,' said my wise mother. 'They have to work for free.'

I called up Muzammal to play one of the two brothers.

'I don't really have a lot of time right now,' he said. 'My friend Jawad and I are training for a kickboxing fight.'

'Bring him,' I replied. 'He can play your brother.'

'But we don't really look like brothers.'

'Doesn't matter. You're both brown so it'll work.'

'I don't know, we have a tournament in two days . . . '

'Ummi says you have to help me.'

'Fine, but you only have two hours.'

'You should try the mosque,' said my mother. But I needed white people, so I decided to try my luck with the neighbours. A burly-looking man was cutting his lawn across the street, so I went and introduced myself. His name was Bret, which he had helpfully tattooed in large script on his forearm.

'How'd you like to be in my film?' I asked.

'No one's ever asked me to act before,' he said. 'It doesn't require any nudity, does it?'

'It's not porn. It's about Muslim stereotypes. I'm looking for someone to play a police officer.'

'Like Bruce Willis in *Die Hard*?'

'Exactly like Bruce Willis,' I replied, never having seen any of the *Die Hard* movies.

'Cool. You could make porn with the same title.'

I was wondering if I should have gone to the mosque like my mother told me.

'Do I get a real police-officer costume?'

'Of course.' I mentally noted that I would need costumes.

'Can you get me the kind where the pants rip off?'

'You're a police officer, not a stripper. But I may only be able to afford the hat,' I said. 'We'll just shoot you from the neck up.'

A few doors down, an elderly man was playing checkers with his grandson on the porch. I introduced myself and learned his name was Tom. I explained that I was making a visionary short film that focused on the delicate balance of race relations.

'Can my wife be in your movie too?' asked Tom when I offered him the coveted role of Neighbour No. 1.

'Sure. The more the merrier.'

'And my grandson. He's staying with us while his parents are vacationing in Cuba.'

I looked at the little boy. He seemed excited by the idea of being an extra.

'They can all be in it,' I replied.

I needed a crowd scene for when the barbecue blows up.

'Are you supplying costumes?' asked Tom.

What was it with the costumes?

'I love what you're wearing now,' I said, staring at his trousers. 'Did you buy those at Hugo Boss?'

'No, Value Village,' he replied.

'We can't compete with that. Would you be willing to wear them for the shoot?'

He agreed, and after a few more uneventful recruitments I had just one role left: the Reporter. I was getting a little desperate and contemplating the idea of my mother in pale face powder when I spied a neighbour coming home from work.

'Excuse me,' I said.

'Oh, I'm happy being a Christian,' said the woman as she unpacked groceries from her car. 'But I heard that a Moonie family moved into number fifty-five – maybe they'd be interested in converting?'

I realized that I had a script in my hand.

'Oh no, I'm not a proselytizer,' I replied. 'I'm a director casting for a film, and you'd be perfect for the role of the Reporter.'

'Really, me?'

'Yeah, the moment I saw you, I knew,' I said, since what I was looking for was someone who had a pulse and both eyes aimed in reasonably the same direction.

'I always wanted to act, but my mother discouraged it,' she said. 'She said I needed a real job, because actresses have to sleep their way to the top.'

'Well, you don't have to have sex with me to get this role. Plus I'm terrible in bed.' I didn't really know why I was going down this road.

'I could teach you a few things,' she said.

'I'll keep that in mind. See you tomorrow afternoon.'

I returned home triumphant.

'Did you find enough people?' asked my mother.

'Yep. But you have some strange neighbours.'

'They're all white. What do you expect?'

'Do you think that Aunty Noreen would let us shoot the film in her house?'

'What's so great about her house?' asked my mother, rather snidely.

'What do you have against her?' I regretted the question immediately.

'She buys store-bought samosas and passes them off as her own.'

'Well, samosas are hard to make,' I said, trying to appeal to her sense of practicality.

'And once she gave me a bag of her old shalwar kameez, as if I'm some sort of charity case. But the worst was when she gave your father her home-made mango chutney. That's too fresh if you ask me.'

'But her house is amazing,' I said. 'It's full of antiques and hardwood. The more expensive the house, the more expensive the film looks. It'll seem like we had a budget.'

'I doubt the antiques are real. They're probably replicas made in China, like her samosas.'

'Please just call her,' I begged my mother.

Two hours later, we sat on an overstuffed chintz sofa in Aunty Noreen's perfectly appointed living room as she served us suspiciously perfect samosas on fine bone china. My mother gave me a knowing look.

'Of course you can use my house, darling,' said Aunty Noreen. 'What are friends for?'

'You're the best, Aunty,' I said, as the final piece in my film fell into place.

Aunty Noreen picked up my script from the coffee table.

'You know I got the lead for a big Bollywood film shooting in my home town when I was just eighteen years old?'

'Really? I didn't know you were a Bollywood star.'

'It fell through. My mother arranged my marriage for that very weekend and I had to back out. I would have been bigger than Aishwarya Rai,' said Aunty Noreen.

'I'm sure Aishwarya couldn't believe her good fortune,'

said my mother, sipping her tea. Aunty Noreen ignored her.

'If you wanted, I could play the brother, except of course I'd be the sister.'

'You're just a little bit . . . ' I didn't know how to be diplomatic about her age.

'You can play the grandmother,' said my mother as she warily picked up a samosa. 'Sorry, I spoke too soon. You're not the right age for the grandmother. Great-grandmother would be more appropriate.'

'Do you want my house or not?' said Aunty Noreen, ignoring my mother.

'I guess—'

'We don't want your house, you wrinkled old roti,' said my mother, slamming down her cup. 'And these samosas aren't even filled with meat, they're full of dried-up peas, like your house.'

'Let's not be so hasty,' I told my mother. 'Or so mean.'

'Your mother's never been able to afford hardwood,' said Aunty Noreen. 'It's only ever been shag carpets for her.'

'Your hardwood is the reason you need knee replacements,' retorted my mother as she dragged me out of the door.

'We'll use my house,' she said on the way home. 'Not every film needs a fancy house. Look at the house in *Jungle Fever*.'

'That was a crack house,' I replied.

'And my house is much nicer,' said my mother.

'Action!' I yelled the next afternoon.

'Do we get to rehearse first?' asked my brother.

'No, we don't have the time,' I said. 'Bret needs to get back to his bartending gig in about twenty minutes so we have to hurry. Plus we only have enough film for one take. Action!'

Jawad and Muzammal stood outside my parents' house in their shalwar kameez, acting frightened by the crowd of neighbours gathering around them. It was a Muslim witch-hunt.

'Islam means "peace". We have to pray five times a day – we don't have time for violence,' Jawad told the Reporter.

'Damn those bloody camel jockeys. We should never have let you into this country,' said Neighbour No. 1, in a stunning turn that would have made Meryl Streep proud.

'We should cut off your ears like they do in Saudi Arabia,' said Neighbour No. 2 while slapping his hands emphatically on his pants.

'No, no, we cut off hands, but we have very strict rules for that. For example, if a thief stole because they were hungry . . . ' said Muzammal.

The actor playing Neighbour No. 4 turned round. 'I'm really not feeling it,' she said.

'Don't stop to analyse the script,' I yelled. 'We don't have the time.'

'I can't do my best work if I'm not given context.'

'But you don't have any lines,' I said, flabbergasted.

'Does Saudi Arabia know you're making fun of them?'

'I'm not making fun of them, I'm making fun of the whole issue of cutting off hands.'

'Actually, I'm giving it context,' said Muzammal.

'I have to get back to work in fifteen minutes,' said Bret.

I knew how Spielberg must have felt.

'Your actors were a little wooden,' said Mario on the phone.

'The neighbours,' I said. 'Yeah, Bret ended up bailing on me so we had to use Neighbour No. 3. And I had to give the

Reporter role to Neighbour No. 4 to get her to stop analysing the script.'

'They weren't real actors?'

'Did you think they were?'

'I just thought they were really bad.'

'I had a day's notice to pull the whole thing together,' I said. 'According to my instructor, no one's ever finished the assignment before.'

'Congratulations on being the first.'

'Do you think I should submit it to the Student Academy Awards competition?'

'No.'

'You're a little judgemental,' I said, trying not to feel discouraged.

'Actually, I'm a realist. So are you coming to the festival? Because believe it or not, we have press who would like to meet you.'

I looked at my girls. It wasn't the greatest timing, but then it never really would be.

'I'll be there.'

When Sami came home from work I was upstairs, with Inaya in the crook of my arm, looking at my maternity wardrobe and trying to figure out if there was something appropriate for a film festival. Maysa sat nearby on the toilet, refusing to expel anything.

'You smell terrible,' he said to me. 'Like curdled milk.'

I had forgotten to change my clothes. He held Inaya as I peeled off my shirt. I told him about *BBQ Muslims* getting into the film festival.

'But I won't be able to come with you to Toronto,' he said. Sami was starting a psychiatry residency and we were soon to move to Calgary. He couldn't take time off at this point.

'How are you going to handle two kids alone?' he asked, worried.

'Who said I'll be alone?'

I called my mother.

'Guess what?' I said.

'You're coming for another visit.' A year ago, I had stayed for two weeks with Maysa in tow, making and editing *BBQ Muslims*. She had kept Maysa busy while I was busy. And now I would be back with another baby. She knew the routine by now.

'I miss you and really want to see you,' I said.

'Don't give me that,' she said. 'This is work-related.'

'My film got into the festival. I just need to come for two screenings in September.'

'Is Maysa potty-trained yet?'

'Of course,' I lied.

'And Inaya drinks milk from a bottle?'

'Since the day she was born.'

I flew to Toronto with the girls the day before the screening. I pumped as much milk as possible and stored it in the fridge.

'Don't be long,' said my mother as I left.

I was ushered into a cinema with five other filmmakers whose films had been put into the same group as mine. The theatre was small but seemed opulent. There was tea and coffee in urns that looked like they were made of gold and silver. I was carefully pouring myself an Earl Grey when someone came up behind me.

'You made it,' said Mario, a suave-looking man with a well-manicured goatee and a black Italian suit. He shook my hand and gave me a badge to wear so I could access the other screenings.

'Do you smell curdled milk?' he asked, looking around.

'It's the cream. It's gone bad.' I dashed into the women's washroom to switch my breast pads, which were soaked. I'd forgotten to bring another pair, so I stuffed my bra with reams of toilet paper. I put some more between my bra and my shirt for extra insurance.

My film played just before another short film, *Bangs*, a comedy about the Chinese Canadian community by Carolynne Hew. I introduced myself to her.

'So we've both made comedies about our cultural communities,' she said to me.

'Mine is less a comedy and more an examination of social behaviour,' I said.

As my film unspooled, though, the audience laughed at all the wrong places. I had meticulously hand-drawn the pictures of the two Muslim brothers for the WANTED ad. My intention had been for the pictures to look like the ones in the *Toronto Star* that had inspired the film in the first place. Those photographs had broken my heart when I saw them, and now my rendering of them was making people laugh. But as I watched Jawad and Muzammal clearly overacting and hamming up my dialogue, it finally dawned on me. My film was really cheesy. In fact it was so over-the-top that it seemed I had done it on purpose. I had inadvertently made a satire about terrorism.

Mario took us into the press room, where reporters wanted to talk to us about our films.

'Why did you choose satire as your genre?' asked one.

'"Choose" wouldn't be the right word,' I replied.

'What word then?'

'I'd say I stumbled upon the genre. This is my first film, and I hadn't really figured out my tone yet.'

'Well, your tone turns out to be comedic,' said the reporter.

Mario came up to me.

'Your mother's on the phone,' he said.

'Is everything OK?' I asked her.

'Maysa refuses to sit on the toilet.' My mother was very annoyed.

'She has some issues with the toilet.' Like she won't use it.

'And Inaya won't drink milk from her bottle,' said my harried mother.

I could hear blood-curdling screaming over the phone.

'She's starving and you have to come home now or, I swear to Allah, I will never look after another one of your babies again.'

'Mario, I have to leave.'

'There's a television reporter who wants to do an interview with you.'

I looked down at my shirt. Milk was leaking down the front on to my pants – and pieces of wet toilet paper had started falling out of my blouse. Mario moved his expensive shoes away from me.

'Are you OK?' he asked, aghast.

'I have a four-month-old baby at home and my breasts aren't used to being so full. I have to go now.' I grabbed my coat, covered myself up and ran, a lactating Cinderella, leaving a trail of wet tissue paper behind me.

The next day Mario called again.

'How are you?' he asked.

'Good. Listen, I wanted to thank you for programming my film. It must have taken a lot of courage. I finally realized that it is bit – a lot – amateur.'

It was as close as I could come to self-awareness. I heard a sigh on the other end.

'But it did have a certain quality to it,' said Mario. 'One wanted it to succeed despite its . . . deficiencies.'

It was as close as he could come to praise.

'There are some reporters who still want to talk to you,' he said.

'I'm going home this afternoon,' I said. 'Can they do it over the phone?'

'Sure. So, what are you going to do next?'

'Figure out how to toilet-train a stubborn two-year-old,' I said as I swatted a diaper-clad Maysa.

'No, I mean for your career.'

'I haven't had time to think for about four months now.'

'I have a suggestion.'

'I'm listening.'

'Apply for funding from arts councils. Make another film but with real actors and a real crew next time,' he said. 'And get some professional childcare.'

A few months later Sami and I were watching TV in our new house in Calgary and there was a story about Taslima Nasrin, the Bengali writer. She'd just been issued a fatwa by some extremists.

'Muslims can be so narrow-minded,' I said to Sami.

'Don't be too hard on us,' he said.

'I want to make a film about fatwas and death,' I said. 'It's ripe for a satire.'

'If you say so,' said Sami.

If I could complete a script and get all the funding in time, I'd be able to submit the film for the 1998 Toronto International Film Festival, which was in two years.

I took down the calendar and started counting the months backwards.

'What are you doing?'

'I need to still be pregnant when my film screens, so I don't have to deal with a starving baby. Or a trail of soggy Kleenex.'

'We're going to schedule a baby around a film festival?' he said.

'It's the only way to make sure my mother won't get mad. And you' – I shook my finger at Maysa – 'are going to learn to use the potty.'

'Don't like the potty,' said Maysa, running away.

'Are you sure you want another baby?' asked Sami. 'Because our lives are pretty crazy with these two.'

Inaya vomited all her milk over me. Again.

'Ugh, why does she always do that?' I asked, sighing, and gave the baby to Sami. I went upstairs to change.

The phone rang. It was Mario. He was angry. As usual.

'Now what's wrong, Mario?' I asked as I peeled off my blouse.

'You moved, and didn't leave me a forwarding number.'

'Oh yeah, sorry about that,' I said, feeling sheepish. 'My brother gave you the number again.'

'Yes, we're keeping his number in our database. He seems to be the stable one in your family.

'You have some reporters who want to talk to you,' he said. 'Promise me you'll be at this number for the next few days?'

'I promise.' I pulled on a clean T-shirt. I could swear the stink of rotting milk had sunk into my skin. 'Mario, can I ask you a question?'

'Sure.'

'Do you think I have what it takes to become a film-maker?' I asked, feeling a little vulnerable.

'You do need something that you don't presently have. So I'm going to mail you a gift,' said Mario.

'What is it?'

'Some perfume.'

Coming Full Circle on Circumcision

I held my newborn son for the first time. He was rounder and calmer than his sisters but had the same intoxicating odour of a newborn. He was a healthy ten pounds, which had been a more challenging delivery than the girls. As I admired him, I noticed something amiss.

'Sami, look at his penis. It's deformed – like a worm. Did you know your family had this genetic defect, because none of the men in my family have it?'

My husband looked at me with incredulity for a moment. 'That is what an uncircumcised penis looks like,' he said drily.

'Really?' I knew Muslim men were circumcised but had never seen an uncircumcised penis, since all the penises in my life were Muslim. 'I just gave birth to my very first uncircumcised penis,' I said.

Maysa and Inaya came into the hospital room to see their new brother. Inaya was instantly jealous, so I gave the baby to Sami while I held her. Maysa watched Sami change Rashad's diaper. 'His belly button is in the wrong place,' said Maysa, in awe of his oddly placed anatomy.

My mother, who had come to Calgary for the last month of my pregnancy, however, was not in awe.

'Book the circumcision right away,' she said.

'But we don't circumcise *girls*,' I tried to argue.

'Girls is wrong, boys is right.'

'Can we at least talk about it?'

'You can talk about it all you want,' said my mother. 'But he's getting circumcised.'

I was worried. I'd heard horror stories.

'Maha told me that her friend's great-uncle's third-cousin-once-removed had his penis charred like a hot dog roasted too long on a campfire,' I told Sami, trying to get him on board with at least rethinking the whole process. A newborn's penis is tiny and delicate, and there's not a lot of room for mistakes.

But he had been circumcised and he wasn't worried.

'The process is pretty simple,' he said. 'It's very rare for things to go wrong.'

The hospital recommended Dr Weiner, who was one of the best circumcision men in the city. As soon as we entered the office, his secretary pounced.

'The doctor's name is pronounced "Wayner", not "Weener",' she told me helpfully. Wayner, wayner, wayner. I repeated the name several times in my head so I wouldn't screw it up. But all I could think of was burnt wieners.

She took us into the doctor's office, where I was instructed to remove Rashad's diaper and give him liquid Tylenol. I took a mental picture of the worm penis, which I was getting very attached to.

A kind-looking doctor entered the room.

'Hello, my name is Dr Weiner,' he said.

'Have you ever lost a penis?' I asked pensively.

'I'm sorry about my wife,' said Sami.

'No worries. I get this a lot. No, I've never lost a penis on my watch, and he won't feel any pain,' he answered patiently, clearly used to hysterical mothers worried about their infant sons' tiny bits.

Dr Weiner pulled out a small metal device that looked like a guillotine for a mouse.

'Are you sure that device won't accidently take off the tip of his penis? Because it doesn't look very safe to me. How about we try it out on you first?'

Sami and the doctor looked at me, and then each other.

'Did I apologize for her before?' asked Sami.

'I'm used to it,' said Dr Weiner. 'But she's obviously very nervous, so maybe she should wait outside.'

'I can hear the both of you and I'm staying,' I said. As Dr Weiner got the device ready to circumcise my son, I closed my eyes. 'Ouch!' I yelled in sympathy.

'I haven't started yet,' said the doctor.

I had one more baby boy, who was also circumcised. A few years later, Sami and I were watching *Bones*, but I was distracted. I had read an article in the newspaper and didn't quite know how to bring it up. I was trying to focus on the maggots eating the dead body, but my mind kept wandering back to delicately framing the question. Finally I blurted, 'Do you feel like you were mutilated?'

'What?' asked a flabbergasted Sami, pausing the show.

'Your penis. Do you feel like you were sexually mutilated? I read this article about a man who felt that since his foreskin was removed as a baby he never had a chance to consent. He felt mutilated and says his sex life is crap.'

Sami sighed. 'My sex life is great.'

'Yeah, mine's OK too.' Sami looked at me. 'I mean, it's *great.*'

'Good.' Sami turned the TV back on.

'If you want, you could wear weights on your penis and restretch the foreskin. Things wouldn't be exactly the same as before, but . . . '

Sami pressed the pause button again. 'I don't feel mutilated. I never think about it, and I'd really like to stop talking about it.' He turned the show back on.

'But what if our boys think they've been mutilated? What are we going to tell them?'

'It's never going to occur to them unless you keep talking about it.'

I mulled this over for a while, wondering where you would attach penis weights to exactly. Did they come with miniature clamps? Wouldn't that pinch?

'Sami, can I take a quick look at your penis to see if the weights would be even possible? I don't think there's enough skin left to attach them.'

'Do not attach anything to my penis. And if you keep talking, I'm turning this off and we're watching the late-night news.'

'So you're not taking off your pants?'

'NO!'

I could see why Muslim men have a reputation for being mean.

We went back to watching *Bones*, where I was sure that Seeley, being a practising Catholic, would approve of circumcision. Neither male nor female circumcision is mentioned in the Qur'an. There are stories that the male prophets of God were circumcised and that's where the tradition came from. But they also lived in a desert area without a lot of water, so

I imagined it was also a convenience thing. Sami could tell I wasn't focusing on the show. He sighed and paused it again.

'Trust me, if men felt circumcision was affecting their sexuality in a negative way, we would not allow anyone to touch our penises. As a gender, we may repress women, but we take care of our own.'

I decided he was right and let go of the topic.

As we ate lasagne the next night our son Zayn was especially excited.

'Guess what I found out today?'

'You're a dufus?' suggested Inaya. But he was too elated to let his older sister get to him.

'My friends said they have to pull back this piece of skin before they pee, and I told them I didn't have anything to pull back.'

The foreskin had come home to roost. I cleared my throat and gave Sami a look. I was going to handle this.

'You used to look like a worm,' I told the boys. 'Your penises, I mean.'

'And what happened?' they asked.

'We circumcised you,' I said, with worry.

'So we weren't born like this?' asked Rashad.

'Like mother, like son,' said Sami.

'But you're OK with that, right?' I said.

'Oh please, who cares if he's not OK with it?' said Inaya, rolling her eyes. 'If you didn't remove it, their penises would get all black from infections and fall off.'

'That can happen?' said Zayn.

'No, it can't,' said Sami. 'If you had a foreskin, you'd have to make sure it was always clean.'

'Yeah, right,' said Inaya. 'They don't even wash their faces or brush their teeth. Like they're gonna do that.'

'What do you mean they don't brush their teeth?' I asked in alarm. 'When was the last time you brushed your teeth?' I asked Zayn.

'I did it last week,' he replied proudly.

That evening, while watching *Heroes*, I had an epiphany.

'If we hadn't circumcised the boys, what would that have meant?'

'We would have had to teach them to pull back their foreskins and clean underneath,' said Sami, with his finger on the pause button.

'Couldn't do it,' I said. 'It's bad enough finding their lunches after a whole summer of decay. Cleaning out their foreskins too – forget it.'

'But what if they grow up and feel like they've been mutilated?' he said.

'I'll buy them miniature weights to regrow their foreskins.'

'So you've come full circle on your opposition to circumcising the boys?' said Sami, finger still hovering over the pause button.

'Totally over it. I'm never going to talk about it again.'

'Good,' said Sami.

That was when the two boys came downstairs, looking triumphant.

'OK, we feel that we are owed reparations for things done to us without our consent,' said Zayn.

'Do you know what "reparations" even means?' asked Sami.

'We Googled it,' said Rashad, pulling out a piece of paper. 'It means redress for gross and systematic violations of human law.'

'And we feel removing our foreskins was totally gross, so we want reparations in the form of money,' said Zayn.

'Really, you want to be compensated for the removal of your foreskins?' said Sami.

'No, we just want money,' said Rashad.

'Or the equivalent in candy,' added Zayn.

'OK, how about this? According to your mother, foreskins can be regrown,' said Sami.

'Really?' said the boys in unison.

'Yep, I'm going to attach binder clips to your penises and hang some Wii remote controllers for weights, and in a couple of months you'll have foreskins again.'

'That sounds like it might hurt,' said Zayn.

'No pain, no gain.'

The boys looked at each other.

'Can we just get five dollars each?' asked Rashad.

'What are you going to buy?' I asked as Sami handed each boy a bill.

'Gummy worms,' said Zayn.

It worked for me.

Water Jug Blues

You know how Catholics have guilt about sin? Muslims have guilt about unwashed private parts. It's almost pathological, really. We buff our twigs and berries and muffins as if they were the hood ornaments of an expensive European car. It gives new meaning to the phrase 'polishing the family jewels'.

As a result, every Muslim household worth its salt and clean giblets has some sort of pouring vessel beside the toilet. And this vessel needs to be filled at a sink, preferably within seated reaching distance. This crucial feature is what brought me to haul Zayn, when he was an eight-month-old, up the stairs of my then partially built house in Regina, to talk to a man we'll call Doug, the supervising contractor, who was conveniently standing in my unfinished washroom. He sighed as he looked at me.

'I'm back,' I said cheerfully.

'Yeah,' said Doug unenthusiastically.

Doug had the unenviable job of building new houses for

our family and for Sami's mom and dad side by side on a lot we'd bought in the south end of Regina. I had been harassing Doug with various requests over the last few weeks. He wanted to finish this house and never see me again. I was a pain in his dubiously washed ass.

My previous requests, I admit, had been idiotic. Could the roof be super-pointy, like the Hansel and Gretel house? Apparently not, since it would involve danger pay for the roofers, not to mention the house wasn't designed that way. Or could the electric sockets be in the middle of the walls so I wouldn't have to bend down to plug in the vacuum cleaner? After all, Doug gave my father-in-law an electric socket in the middle of *his* wall next door so he could plug in a giant framed photograph of the Kaaba that he bought during the hajj. The picture was a masterpiece of Islamic kitsch, showing not just the Kaaba itself but the surrounding buildings, complete with tiny red and yellow lights built into the four minarets, which blinked on and off continuously.

'That picture is the height of tackiness. Should you really be encouraging my father-in-law to have it up on his wall?' I asked Doug when he hung it up.

'It's his picture. If he likes it, he can put it up.'

'But the blinking lights are a violation of the health code,' I insisted.

'How's that possible?' asked Doug.

'I feel an epileptic seizure coming on whenever I look at it.'

Doug just ignored me. He listened to my father-in-law as if he were God, but ignored me like the irritating patron saint of stubbed toes: no sale on my vacuum-cleaner sockets or fairy-tale roof.

In all honesty, it was a good thing that he stopped listening to my attempts to build a house that resembled something out of the Brothers Grimm. I had obsessed over home décor magazines and tried to use their ideas, to mixed, mostly disastrous results. Why couldn't an accent-wall colour match an accent-grout colour? I picked out a dark orange grout for the tiled floor upstairs, which unfortunately dried to the same fluorescent hue as the school bus that picks up my kids. Doug was forced to meticulously paint over it with a coloured sealant so he wouldn't have to rip out the entire floor. By the time I mounted those stairs with Zayn in my arms, he was at the end of his tether.

But this time my request was a serious one. From the time we are infants, Muslim children are taught to sit calmly on the commode while doing our business, use toilet paper for number two, and then rigorously wash our private parts by pouring water from the jug that's always conveniently sitting by the toilet. And yes, even the boys have to sit while peeing. White people may say that Islam is a backward religion, but the Sharia got our men to sit on a toilet and we're keeping this one because it saves our bathrooms. Religion has its uses.

Squeaky-clean butts are mandatory for everyone, as are pristine penises or vaginas, depending on your circumstances. It is part of *fitra* – keeping fingernails, toenails, armpit hair, pubic hair and moustaches short. (The final requirement is just for men, although advisable for women as well.) I needed Doug not to dismiss me this time.

'I need the toilet right next to the sink.'

'That's where they usually go,' he replied.

'Yeah, but I need to be able to reach the tap while I'm sitting on the toilet.'

I didn't want to elaborate, but it was obvious he wasn't

taking me seriously. I knew I'd have to tell him the truth, but I felt like I was confessing some deep, dark secret, like that I had an extra belly button. I finally decided the best way was to just blurt it out.

'We wash our butts with water after, you know, we use them, and I need to be able to fill my jug with water while I'm on the toilet. Getting up and walking to another corner of the bathroom with my underwear around my ankles is kind of awkward.'

Doug looked at me for a while. I knew what he was thinking. It was a bad economy and this was a paying gig, weird religion notwithstanding. But he was horrified. I understood how he felt. When I was little I asked my parents why white people didn't have jugs beside their toilets. Because they don't use water, I was told. Well, what do they use? After toilet paper, nothing. It was just better not to think about it. Doug broke my reverie.

'Why don't you just order a toilet that can wash all your parts?' he asked.

It was an astute question.

'I don't trust those toilets. What if you press the wrong button and get a blast of hot water? Your butt is a delicate organ.'

'How far do you want the sink from the toilet?' he asked wearily.

Victory. Handily, I'd brought a jug along for a demonstration. But I was holding a baby, so Doug squatted on the pretend toilet and held the jug out towards the future sink. He pretended he was turning on the tap and filling the jug and then moved it back to his crotch.

'Good for you?' he asked me.

'Yes, that's great,' I said. Doug followed my gaze. I was

staring at his crotch, though in my defence he had a jug spout pointing straight at it.

'I mean the jug, not your ...' Doug removed the jug quickly from his crotch; trouble like this, he didn't need. How would he even explain a situation like this to the Contractors' Union's Sexual Harassment Hotline? 'So, tell us again why you were pointing a water jug at your crotch?' I tried to change the subject.

'Growing up, we used a plastic container, the kind that they sell in the dairy aisle to hold milk or pour juice.'

'Those are good plastic jugs,' replied Doug, glad to be on neutral territory again.

'Yeah, but sometimes the jug got mistaken for its original purpose. One time, my husband went to a potluck dinner at the mosque and they were serving grape Kool-Aid in the same plastic jugs that they used in the outhouses at Muslim summer camp,' I said.

'You guys should label your jugs more carefully,' he replied, obviously making a note not to eat at mosque potlucks.

'They had MYG, for "Muslim Youth Group", written on them with black Magic Marker, but I guess that wasn't specific enough. In retrospect they should have labelled them GENITAL CLEANING JUGS or something like that.'

My husband has never fully recovered. 'It was horrible,' he says with the same revulsion twenty-odd years later.

'That's probably the most disgusting thing I've ever heard,' replied Doug.

That got my back up. How dare he, the non-ass-washer, criticize our imbibing habits?

'To be fair, the jug doesn't actually come into contact with – you know. It just pours water over ... them, so the pain was mostly psychological on his part.'

There was an uncomfortable silence. Doug looked at the jug in his hand.

'I like this jug. It has a spout,' he replied.

'Yeah, for sure they have better aim. The only thing you have to be careful about is impalement.' This is probably why Muslims don't drink alcohol; we can't afford to lose our hand-eye-genital dexterity.

'Some Muslims saw off the spout, like white people saw off the barrel of a shotgun,' I tell Doug. 'But I consider that the height of unsophistication. Like, only brown trash do things like that. How are you going to explain green plastic splinters stuck in your penis to an emergency doctor?'

'You could say you were in a rush,' offered Doug.

'Washing one's genitals should never be done in haste. You should take your time, savour the moment.'

Doug said nothing.

'You can never be too careful. I had a friend who used to put boiling water in the communal watering jug to trick her sisters,' I told an increasingly uncomprehending Doug. 'So you always have to be alert for sibling shenanigans. And never chop green chillies just before you wash yourself. I did that once when I was making shrimp and squash curry for my mother-in-law.'

'I bet that burns,' said Doug, thinking over the ramifications.

'For a long time, too. But on a positive note, it got rid of my yeast infection.

'You should try keeping a water jug by your toilet,' I said.

'Someone would just take it,' said Doug.

'Yeah, every summer Sami is usually yelling from the bathroom because the jug is gone. One of the kids uses it to water their plants. It's worse when we travel. I leave my water bottle by the toilet, but the maid always takes it because she thinks it's garbage. Sometimes in hotels we use the Styrofoam coffee cups, but recently I heard a comic named Azhar Usman making a joke about using the coffee pot—'

'What did you say?' asked Doug.

'I said usually we just use a water bottle . . . '

'You use the coffee pot?'

'Well, they are large enough, and they pour really well.'

'I don't think the maids clean the coffee pots.'

'Well, I don't make them dirty.'

'How could you do something like that to other people?'

'It's not like it touches anything really.'

'I do not want to drink coffee from an object that's been down there!' he yelled.

Now it was my turn to be uncomfortable.

'I promise never to use a hotel coffee pot again,' I said as solemnly as I could.

'And tell your friends to stop using them too,' he asked.

'Yes, I'll send out a bulletin to all Muslims right away.'

'Good.' He took me seriously.

White people. We had clearly reached the end of the conversation about genital-washing. At least for adults.

'I was also hoping to wash the baby's . . . just wash the baby, so could you put the hole for the sink a little over to the right so there's enough counter space to lay him down?'

Doug eyed Zayn and then pulled out his measuring tape and impassively measured him. I slapped a changing-pad on the rough plywood counter and rotated Zayn so his diapered nether regions were directly under the future tap. I could tell Doug was more relaxed dealing with the baby's needs than mine. Doug put markings down where the future sink would go as Zayn's legs teetered in the air.

'I just think it's more environmentally friendly to wash the baby under the tap than waste all those pieces of pre-moistened paper.' Then it occurred to me: maybe white people use those pre-moistened towelettes on themselves, which would make sense. I felt I had shamed Doug by implying that his own post-void cleanliness was substan-dard. I thought I'd give him a chance to open up about his habits.

'I'm sure baby wipes could be used by adults too. Have you ever tried it?'

Doug said nothing. OK then. But I could tell he was building to something.

'Do men clean themselves too?' he asked. What a ques-tion.

'Of course. Why wouldn't they?'

'Well, men stand up and then just shake . . . '

'There's no standing for men in Islam, much less shaking it,' I replied with as much indignation as I could muster. 'They sit like the rest of us. The washroom is a democracy.'

'Your men are whipped,' he said.

'In washrooms, for sure.'

Awkward silence.

'The bathtubs just arrived,' Doug said, pointing at several large white plastic tubs with a white wall liner to cover the three walls of the shower area. No tile, no grout (Doug had learned his lesson). The tubs temporarily distracted me. Doug had ordered them without consulting me. Probably to reduce the chance of being forced to communicate.

I suddenly remembered a new cleaning issue related to the bathtubs.

'Muslims have to take a ritual bath after sex called *ghusl*. We have to wash our whole body, not just our ... sexual organs.' But Doug had vanished. I should have just stuck with bum-washing.

The Packing Crate

'Turn on the TV,' said Sabreena. I was cradling the phone under one ear while washing baby food off Zayn's face under the tap in the kitchen.

'What's up?' I said. 'Are the Patriots playing?' Sabreena and her family had moved to Boston at the beginning of September.

'*Turn on the TV.*'

'Fine,' I sighed, and grabbed the remote. As I saw the plane go into the tower, the words 'Please don't let it be us' played over and over again in my brain.

The reporter mentioned a Muslim connection. I got a little woozy and put down Zayn, who crawled away to play with some toy cars. I had to remind myself that I wasn't involved. I'd been home all day, plus I didn't know how to fly a plane. But the feelings of collective guilt and fear were hanging inside me. I hung up with Sabreena, took a few breaths and assessed the situation. I was in Saskatchewan. One-year-old Zayn was obsessing over the wheels on a plastic truck, and the other three children were in school. I checked the clock; it was recess time at Massey School. I knew the girls would be running around playing with their friends, all of whom knew they were Muslim. Religion didn't make any difference in the playground. But I just had to be sure. I called the school secretary, who was very patient with me.

'The children are safe here,' she said kindly. 'There's nothing to worry about.'

'Just please send someone out and make sure they're OK,' I insisted.

'Well, it's recess, but I'll go check.'

A few minutes later, she called me back.

'They're fine. Maysa says she's sorry about trading her chicken curry sandwich for a Rice Krispie Square. And Inaya says Breanne deserved the punch.'

I was relieved. They were up to their usual childhood antics.

'We would let you know right away if someone said anything to them,' said the secretary, reading my mind.

I thanked her and hung up. I spent the rest of the morning staring at the TV and fretting. The only time I could tear myself away was to set out a bowl of Cheerios so Zayn wouldn't starve to death. What would the neighbours think of us? Would they be worried about living beside the only Muslim family on the block? The phone rang.

'This is South Albert Montessori School,' said the woman. 'I've got Rashad here with me in the office. Are you coming to get him? He's been waiting for about half an hour and is very upset.'

'I'll be right there.' I threw the remote on to the sofa. 'Damn it,' I said to Zayn as I buckled him into his car seat and drove to the preschool. Rashad was playing with blocks while his teacher watched him.

'I'm so sorry,' I said, scooping him up and burying my nose in his hair. 'These terrorists flew a plane into towers in New York, which I had nothing to do with, and I got totally engrossed in the news.'

'I heard. Everyone's a bit off today,' said the teacher. 'While you're here, though, did you happen to bring Rashad's permission slip for our field trip?'

Crap. 'Um, no. I'm so sorry, with all the horrible things that are happening today, I completely forgot.'

'It was due last week,' she said gently. 'But I have some forms here for you to sign.' She handed me some sheets of paper. 'And let's get signatures for the rest of Rashad's trips this term.' I quickly signed the papers. Smart teacher. Despite the world's calamities, she still had to get her students to the science centre and the petting zoo.

As soon as we got home, I dumped some crayons and paper on the squat plastic play table, as well as a bag of potato chips and some gummy worms, to keep the boys quiet while I obsessed in front of the TV. Canada was my only home, but I felt as if something had changed. With the death count numbering in the sickening thousands, I knew nothing could go back to the way it was before.

When Sami came home I pounced while he was still putting his coat away. I made sure Zayn and Rashad couldn't hear us.

'Life as we know it is over,' I said, completely panicked.

'You're overreacting,' said Sami as he looked at the boys. Zayn's head was in the potato-chip bag, where he was licking the salt off the inside of the foil. Sami removed the bag. Rashad was picking gummy worms out of his hair and eating them.

'You're underreacting,' I replied.

'I think people can distinguish us from terrorists.' Sami brushed crumbs off both boys.

'People are really angry with Muslims right now,' I said. 'They are not going to forgive us.'

'*We* didn't do anything wrong, so we don't need their forgiveness. Let's turn this off,' said Sami, gently uncurling my fingers from the remote. I heard the school bus pull up. Maysa and Inaya stomped into the house. I quickly ran over to them to make sure they weren't traumatized by the attacks. I enveloped them in a big hug. They pushed me away.

'How can you see us in the playground?' asked Maysa, angry. 'I had to give back the Rice Krispie Square. You never make those.'

'Those things are just air,' I said. 'I'm giving you real food.'

'Why does Maysa think you can see her from the house?' asked Sami.

'It's because Mama can see through brick,' Inaya said nonchalantly. 'Breanne deserved her punch. But the principal said I can't hit her any more. When Mama takes a shower can she still see us?'

Sami looked at me.

'I'm going to make sure your parents are OK,' I said, and headed next door. My mother-in-law was on the phone with Sabreena. I could tell she was worried about her daughter. Two days ago, Sabreena had flown to the States with her three kids to join her husband, Amir, who was starting a post-doc at Harvard. The move was so recent that a white packing crate full of their things was still sitting in her parents' driveway, waiting to be picked up by the movers. My mother-in-law gave me the phone.

'Are you OK? I don't think it's a good idea to live in the US right now,' I told Sabreena.

'It's bad timing,' she replied, 'but we have to get on with our lives.' Sabreena and I were really close, and I already missed her. With that day's panic in the air, I wanted her home.

'I think it's safer in Canada,' I said as I watched my father-in-law come home from the office where he worked as an ear, nose and throat doctor. He put his briefcase down and untied his shoes.

'You're late,' said my mother-in-law.

'I was meeting with an RCMP officer,' he said.

'What?' I asked, instantly alarmed.

'He came to see me at work. One of the neighbours saw the packing cube on the driveway and thought it was a little suspicious.'

'Did you hear that, Sabreena?' I barked, putting her on speakerphone.

'He just wanted to know why it was there,' replied my father-in-law.

My worst fears had just come to life. The neighbours were turning against us.

'Well, this is a difficult time,' Sabreena reasoned. 'Maybe people just need some reassurance.'

'The neighbour could have just knocked on the door for reassurance,' I said. 'I don't call the RCMP if I want to know why a neighbour bought a new car.'

'Obviously they were worried,' said my father-in-law, looking as tired as I'd ever seen him.

'They're worried that we have a link to the towers,' I said, growing more paranoid.

'You live in Saskatchewan,' said Sabreena. 'It's not exactly a hotbed for unrest. I mean, maybe the wheat farmers get a bit riled up when it rains during harvest season, but other than that you're a peaceful province.'

'Exactly,' I said. 'Your parents have lived peacefully in Saskatchewan for over forty years, and now in the blink of an eye people are frightened of them.'

'Well, we lived on the same street for over thirty years and then we moved,' said my mother-in-law calmly. 'Maybe the new neighbours need time to get to know us better.'

'Sending us a muffin basket is a good way to get to know us better. The RCMP does not deliver muffins!' I may have been frothing a little at the mouth by this point. How could my in-laws not see how horrible this was? 'People think we're a danger to the neighbourhood. Maybe we should move.'

'I thought you said Canada was safer?' said Sabreena.

'Obviously anywhere there's people, there's gonna be a problem,' I said.

'So where do we move?'

'Where there aren't any people.'

'Like the desert,' said Sabreena. 'You'd have to home-school the kids.'

'I could handle that.'

'You lied and told the preschool that Rashad was toilet-trained and put him in a pull-up for almost a year,' said Sabreena. 'You can't handle children at home – you'd go insane.'

My sister-in-law was right. I'd spent the past month finding daycare for Zayn. He was starting the next week. I had too many children and now it was too late to escape to the desert.

'The anxiety will blow over,' said Sabreena. 'Let's just give the neighbours some time.'

'Time to mobilize the neighbourhood so they can round us up and lock us away somewhere.'

My in-laws sat silently. My prophecies for doom and gloom were affecting their mood.

'We can't just give up,' said Sabreena.

I had an idea. We had to become proactive.

'Let's invite the neighbours for a giant open house,' I said.

'So they will be more at ease with us,' said my mother-in-law.

'So we can smoke out the one who called the police,' I said.

I came home to find Sami feeding the kids some vegetables.

'You know I fed them already,' I said.

'Potato chips and Cheerios don't count as dinner,' he said. 'You'll give them diabetes.'

'They're young. They'll bounce back.'

'What are you doing?' Sami asked me as I sat down at the computer.

'I'm making up invitations for an open house at your parents' place. One of the neighbours thinks your father is a terrorist henchman, so I'm trying to figure out who it is.'

'What's a henchman?' asked Inaya.

'Someone involved in criminal activity,' I replied as I typed.

'Could I be a henchman?' she asked.

'With your right hook, probably yes,' I said, typing out my invitation.

'No, you could not,' said Sami, smoothing down her hair. 'You have to stop punching Breanne in the playground.'

'Can you see me from work, too?' asked Inaya.

'We talked about this,' said Sami. 'No one can see you at school unless they're there.'

'Is Dadu involved in bad things?' asked Maysa.

'Nope,' I said, 'but we're gonna find out who is, at the party.'

I examined my simple, straightforward print-out. The phone rang and Sami went to answer it.

'That was my father,' said Sami, getting off the phone. 'He

wants to make it clear that this is a neighbourly get-together and not a witch-hunt.'

'Will there be witches at this party?' asked Inaya.

'Maybe just one,' said Sami, watching me cut and fold my invitations.

There were at least thirty houses in our neighbourhood. I put my coat on because it was already getting cold.

'Where are you going?' asked Sami.

'To hand these out to the neighbours,' I said.

'Why don't you let me do that?'

'Don't you trust me?'

'No,' said Sami.

'What are you afraid Mama will do?' asked Maysa.

'I'm afraid she's going to harass the neighbours,' said Sami.

'I'm not five,' I said. 'I can control my emotions.'

'I'm five and I can control my emotions too,' said Inaya. 'What's an emotion?'

'"Emotion" is a word for feelings,' said Sami.

'Like Mama's feeling a little crazy,' said Maysa.

'Yep,' said Sami.

'Can I come?' asked Inaya.

'No, you have anger-management issues,' I said. 'When you stop hitting people, you can come.' I bundled Rashad into a coat and picked up Zayn.

'You should take a pushchair with you,' said Sami.

'I'll look more maternal if I carry him.'

'You're using our children as props?'

I hauled the kids out the door.

A few houses down, I let Rashad ring the doorbell. An elderly man answered.

'Hi, I'm Zarqa, one of your neighbours,' I said, looking as innocent as I could.

'I'm Dave. I've seen you around with your many children.'

'I love children and bringing life into the world,' I said, patting Zayn's head. 'Aren't kids such a gift?'

Rashad bit my arm. I swatted him on his butt.

'Ouch, Mama hit me,' said Rashad as I pinched him into silence.

'What can I do for you?' said Dave, watching me push Rashad behind me.

'My father-in-law is having an open house, and he'd like to invite you.'

'That's incredibly generous of him.'

'Isn't it?' I replied. 'He just feels that after today's terrible events, it's better to get to know our neighbours so we won't be suspicious of each other.'

'I don't know why anyone would be suspicious of your family,' said Dave.

'I know, right, but someone who lives on this block called the RCMP. You wouldn't know who that was, would you?' I watched Dave closely to see if he betrayed any signs of guilt.

His eyes kept darting over my shoulder. He wouldn't make full eye contact.

'Is there anything you want to tell me, Dave? Because now would be the time.'

'Actually, there is,' he said. 'Your son just took off across the street.'

I looked down and Rashad was gone. I could see him tearing down the block heading for a busy intersection. There was no way I could catch him with Zayn in tow.

I threw Zayn into a startled Dave's arms. Rashad was already out of sight as I ran down the street after him. Jill, another neighbour, spotted him and intercepted him as he ran past her driveway. She held on to him as I came huffing and puffing down the street. By the time I got to her, she had him pacified with a lollipop, which did the trick.

'Crazy day?' she asked.

'Yeah. I stupidly forgot to bring candy with me.' I handed her an invitation to the open house.

'What's this?'

'Someone called the RCMP on my father-in-law, so now my family's having an open house to be all friendly and welcoming,' I said, doubled over because I was having trouble breathing.

'That's really kind of your father-in-law,' said Jill.

'Yeah, I'm pretending I really care too. But I just want to find the bastard. Can you make it?'

'Will there be meatballs?'

'I'll ask my mother-in-law to make some,' I said.

'Count me in.'

Jill handed Rashad over to me. I held tightly to his hand as I returned to Dave's house.

'Thanks, Dave,' I said as I took Zayn from him.

'And thank you for the invitation.'

As I headed up my driveway to the front door, Dave caught up to me. I had dropped Zayn's hat on the street and he handed it back.

'By the way, I wasn't the one who called the RCMP.'

I took the hat and thanked him.

Sami had heard the exchange at the front door.

'You promised not to harass the neighbours,' said Sami.

'I don't know why he said that,' I replied. 'White people.'

'Mama pinched me,' said Rashad, showing his father the red mark on his arm.

'I'll give out the rest of the invitations,' said Sami. 'The last thing we need is the RCMP arresting you for child abuse.'

'We want to come,' said Inaya, getting her sweater. Maysa put on her windbreaker.

As Sami left with Zayn and Rashad in the pushchair, and the girls in tow, I put some water in the kettle for tea. After a few moments of thinking, I dialled the number for our local newspaper.

'*Leader-Post*,' said the reporter on the line.

'Hi, I'd like to report one of my neighbours,' I said.

'This isn't the police,' said the reporter. 'Maybe you should dial 911?'

'No, I mean one of the neighbours reported us to the RCMP, so I think you should investigate who that person was.'

'What did the neighbour report you for?'

'Being involved in today's attacks.'

'The terrorist attacks in New York?' asked the reporter. 'Are you planning to attack here? There isn't much to blow up except for the grain silos. Is that it? Disrupt Canada's wheat distribution? That's ingenious.'

'I wasn't involved,' I said, annoyed. 'A neighbour saw a white packing cube in the driveway and thought it was suspicious. I want you to find out who that neighbour was.'

'I can't help you with that,' said the reporter. 'But this is definitely worth a story.'

'No, wait—' I said, but it was too late. The reporter hung up on me.

The next day a story appeared in the newspaper about how a local Muslim family had been the focus of a police investigation.

'How did they find out about this?' said Sami, unhappy.

'I don't know,' I said. 'Maybe one of your father's patients noticed him being interrogated by the RCMP.'

'This is terrible. A reporter showed up at my father's office asking questions.'

'Well, at least everyone will know the whole story now,' I said. 'Isn't that what we want?'

'We don't want the neighbours to think we're having an open house just to find out who called.'

'But the person who called will know how upsetting it was.'

'And that person probably won't come to the house,' said Sami. 'Because they'll feel like we just want to find them.'

'Or they'll come because they don't want us to suspect that they're avoiding us.'

'So you'll never really know,' said Sami.

I Googled 'polygraph machines'. Turns out you can't get them on a week's notice.

The day of the open house arrived, and the article in the newspaper had aroused everyone's curiosity. As the neighbours filed into the house, I kept an eye out for anyone who looked a little shady.

'Hi,' I said to an old woman trying to pour herself some tea. 'Let me help you.'

'Thank you, dear. My name is Ruth. Did you cook this wonderful food?'

'No, my cooking isn't this good,' I replied, thinking that Ruth looked a little nervous. 'My mother-in-law made it.'

'You're very fortunate to have such a wonderful relationship with your mother-in-law,' she said.

'I know. She won't let me wallow in self-pity.'

'She's right,' replied Ruth. 'More than ever, Muslims need to show themselves as a vital part of society.'

'You're right,' I sighed. 'I'm going to cross you off my list of suspects. You're too nice.'

'She's just joking,' said Sami, suddenly appearing beside me with the girls. I needed to put a bell around his neck so I could hear him coming. Under his breath, he said, 'You promised to be circumspect.'

'What does "circumspect" mean?' asked Inaya.

'Everything your mother is not,' said Sami.

'Look, Rice Krispie squares,' said Maysa, grabbing a bunch and putting them in her mouth.

'I can teach you how to make those, dear,' Ruth told her.

'Mama says they're just air,' said Maysa. 'And that's why white people are good at making them.'

I tried to protest, but Sami pulled me away before I could do more damage.

'I'd like to introduce you to a neighbour I just met.' Sami led me by the elbow towards a salt-and-pepper-haired man. 'Zarqa, this is Brian.'

'Your husband told me that you're quite concerned with improving the reputation of your community. Well, I've got a great idea for you. My church is looking for someone to talk about Islam this Sunday. You'd be perfect.'

'I'm terrible at public speaking. Oh look, we're out of chutney for the samosas,' I said, trying to make a quick getaway, but Sami blocked my escape.

'She's a little rusty, but that's a fantastic idea,' said Sami. 'She should do something more proactive.'

On Sunday, I sat paralysed on the couch. The kids came downstairs dressed for church for the first time in their lives.

'Why are they all coming?' I asked Sami, mortified.

'Because it's good for the kids to see their mother doing something constructive.'

'Can I hold one of the kids for emotional effect?'

'Remember, we didn't have kids to use them as props,' said Sami.

'Maybe you didn't,' I said.

'I don't want to sit beside her,' said Maysa. The other kids concurred.

'Fine, be that way,' I said, looking at them. 'But remember, I brought you into this world, and I can take you out.'

'Please don't say that during your speech,' said Sami.

We packed ourselves into the minivan and left. As soon as we got there, Maysa made a beeline for the snack table, where there were many varieties of Rice Krispie squares.

'I wish Muslims made these,' she said as she devoured three pieces.

Brian introduced me to the congregation as an expert in Islam. I stood at the podium and unfolded some pieces of paper while cursing Sami in my head.

'Thank you for inviting me to your church today. It was really not necessary, given all the other Muslims who live in the city,' I said. 'But since you insisted on having me, I guess I can say a few words.'

'Can you tell us about the five pillars of Islam?' asked Brian.

'Sure. The first pillar is the belief in one god. Which is kind of a thing in religion.'

'Yes, most religions do have a belief in God,' said Brian encouragingly.

'And our second pillar is prayer. We have to pray a lot, five times a day, every day, and some of those times aren't very convenient. Dawn's at 3 a.m. in the summer here. So sleeping in isn't a pillar of Islam, I guess.'

There was an uncomfortable silence. Sami glared at me.

'And the third pillar?' prompted Brian.

'The third pillar is fasting, which we do in the lunar month of Ramadan. It's essentially like Lent if you gave up food and water from dawn to sunset for thirty days. Here's a piece of advice: don't. In the summer, the days are nineteen hours long, and believe me when I tell you that's an ungodly length of time to go without food.'

'But you Muslims do it for very godly reasons,' said Brian. 'Because it reminds you to think about all the hungry and disadvantaged people in this world.'

'So please think of me when I fast,' I said, avoiding Sami's searing gaze. 'And then there's *zakat*, a charitable tax of 2.5 per cent that we pay on our savings to give to the poor. The final pillar is performing the hajj, which means travelling to Mecca in Saudi Arabia and performing all the rituals there at least once in your lifetime. Apparently they don't allow non-Muslims in, but don't take that that as an insult. If we weren't forced to go, we wouldn't either. If you really want sun and sand go to Jamaica instead. It's much more fun, trust me.'

'Thank you for that … umm … wonderful speech,' said Brian, unsure of himself. 'Is there anyone here who'd like to ask a question?'

'Do you slaughter chickens in your bathtub?' asked a man named Charlie. 'Because I heard you do weird voodoo to your animals before you eat them.'

'We say, "*Bismillah, Allahu akbar*," which is voodoo for "In the name of God, God is great", and then slice the jugular with a quick flick of the wrist. It's supposed to be as merciful a death as possible and it renders the meat halal, or acceptable to eat by Muslims.'

'How many chickens have you killed?' asked Charlie.

'None. But there was a time when my father-in-law had to go out to the farm to slaughter his own chickens,' I replied. 'Now we just go to Walmart or to a halal butcher store. So he doesn't need all the equipment at home any more like he used to. But there's nothing suspicious with having that stuff in the basement, because it was only used on animals—'

'Why don't we just stop the talk here,' said Brian, getting red in the face. Great. I'd just told everyone my father-in-law had a slaughterhouse in his basement. If they didn't think we were creepy and weird before . . .

'OK, I have a confession to make,' I said.

'Go on,' said Charlie.

'My sister-in-law was moving to Boston and she had a white packing cube in the driveway and someone thought it was suspicious and called the RCMP to investigate my father-in-law. That phone call really bugs me. But you know what I find most upsetting?'

'That you can't sleep in?'

'Yes – I mean no. I mean that my father-in-law has lived in this neighbourhood for forty years and in one instant some-body erased that entire history.'

Ruth came over to me and held my hand. 'It wasn't you who flew those planes into the towers,' she said. 'You've got to learn to forgive yourself for something you haven't even done.'

'But other people don't forgive,' I said, sulking.

'You can't live your life worrying about other people,' said Ruth. 'Just worry about yourself and raising those little ones. And maybe get a job – something to keep you busy, you know?'

Charlie came up to me.

'I like your religion,' he said. 'It's a little wacky with the headless chickens but it could grow on me. I'd like to convert. Try it out.'

'Charlie, I don't know. We have enough nuts in our com-munity. Do you really want to be a part of that?'

'Ah, people are pretty nuts in these parts too. Plus I always wanted to travel to Mecca. See some Arabs, ride me a camel. What do I have to do? Rub chicken blood on me during a full moon?'

'No, you just go to the mosque and recite the declaration of faith: "There is only God and Muhammad is his messenger."'

'That's it?'

'Yeah, we're kind of minimalist that way,' I said.

That night after we got everyone off to bed, Sami and I cuddled on the couch.

'You did an OK job with the speech,' said Sami.

'You think so?'

'Not really, but my hope is you'll get better with practice. I gave a bunch of people our contact information.'

'Why would you do that? I hate public speaking.'

'Because it's the only way you'll get over your hysteria, and people need to see Muslims speaking, especially women.'

'I hate those hijackers,' I said.

'They have devastated and ruined a lot of people's lives, but not ours,' said Sami.

'We'll never find the neighbour who called the RCMP on us, will we?' I asked Sami. 'I really wanted them to know how wrong they were.'

'I think they already know that and probably feel stupid for ever having called.'

'Do you think the kids will be OK?' I worried about them the most. Their lives would carry the burden of what had happened on September 11th. Their faith would be associated with terror instead of peace. I didn't know how to explain it to them. They were so young.

'Right now their lives revolve around what time recess is,' said Sami.

He was right. The only way they'd been affected by the attacks was through my panic. I felt guilty and wanted to make it up to them. I saw their brown-paper lunch bags on the kitchen counter and got up off the couch.

'What are you doing?' asked Sami.

'I need to make something.' I rooted around in the pantry cupboard, finding my ingredients.

'Now? It's almost eleven.'

'It won't take long,' I said. For children, it was the small things that changed their world for the better. And I could do one small thing tonight.

'What are you making?'

'Rice Krispie squares.'

Behind the Shower Curtain

A giant shower curtain was strung up in the middle of our prayer hall. Muslims have a mania for cleanliness, but this was nuts.

'What would freak out the men more: the water damage,' I said jokingly to Sami, 'or naked women in the mosque?'

The cause of the shower curtain revealed itself as the result of a visiting imam from Saudi Arabia, the land of strangeness. Turns out that the visiting imam felt the men and women should have a physical barrier between them while they prayed. The position of men and women in mosques is a contentious issue. Each mosque differs in its approach to separation, depending on the make-up of the congregation and the architecture of the room. Some spaces of worship mix the two genders in the prayer lines, but those places are in the minority. The majority of mosques separate the genders, either with a physical barrier or by having the women pray in a separate section or behind the men.

In our mosque in Regina, the men prayed in front with the

women behind them. There was no physical barrier between the two groups. Given all the bowing and prostration that goes on in Muslim prayer, the women in our mosque preferred to be the ones at the back, observing the bent-over men. As a female friend said to me once during prayers, 'It's quite a view.'

'In Saudi Arabia, they don't even let women drive,' I said to Sami. 'So why does this man get to influence *our* congregation?'

Saudi Arabia follows a literalist interpretation of Islam called Wahhabism, which I take issue with because their austere rules don't even exist in literature. Descriptions of women riding camels and participating in public life exist in our history of the early Muslim community, and yet Wahhabism outlaws women driving and leaving the house unescorted. To my mind, the Saudis try to mould Islam around their restrictive culture to justify their sexist behaviour. To me, if you're going to be a literalist, then the hadith are clear: women shouldn't be physically restricted in galleries or behind curtains as we are today. We should have the same access to the prayer hall as men.

But the Saudi imam felt differently. The women could be seen too easily by the men during the prayer. What made me crazy was that the men in our mosque didn't dismiss him. Instead, they strung up a shower curtain. I couldn't stomach it. I decided to see if I could convince the imam that he was wrong. I introduced myself, then started with small-talk.

'So, how's the price of oil these days?' (I didn't know any Saudi sports teams.) The imam was shocked that I had approached him. He tried to put some distance between us, but I kept following him. Time to cut to the chase.

'Why are you making us pray behind that thing?' I asked him. 'Isn't it enough that we're behind you guys?'

'It's better for men's concentration if they don't see women.'

'But men don't have eyes in the backs of their heads,' I countered.

'Free mixing of men and women will lead to adultery and fornication and the end of traditional marriage,' he intoned.

'We're already separated and praying in a dignified manner. Don't you think you might be overreacting?'

'Where is your husband?' he asked, desperately looking around.

'What about seeing women in their daily lives?' I asked. 'If men can't concentrate in the mosque, presumably they can't concentrate when they leave their homes. So do they stop functioning in the real world? It's not saying much about men, is it?'

'You have insulted me, and I will no longer speak to you. This is what happens when women speak and walk about freely,' he said to a passing man. 'They get ideas.'

'I'm not praying behind that thing,' I told Sami.

'So don't,' he said.

A few women got together and decided to pray in front of the curtain. Now we were closer than ever to the men.

'This is strangely calm,' I said to Aunty Lubna. The women tended to talk and have children with them. Praying right next to the men was like praying beside a well-disciplined army. They were quiet and didn't trade recipes, such as ketchup mixed with mango chutney makes a great samosa dip.

'It is peaceful,' said Aunty Lubna. 'I could get used to this.' But there was a tension in the air. As men entered the prayer hall, they'd see us sitting in front of the curtain, gape and then keep walking with their heads down.

A few days later, a petition was circulated and the majority of women in the congregation signed it. They wanted the curtain. In the period I now mentally labelled 'Before the Curtain', hardly any women came to the mosque for Friday prayers, but now that everyone wanted to make a point – we love the curtain, we hate the curtain – the place was packed. Our little band continued to pray in front while the majority of women prayed behind, and the Saudi imam fumed because he had inadvertently caused an increase in the visibility of women in the mosque.

I went to the mosque one Wednesday for Maghrib, the sunset prayer. Like Christians who flock to church on Sundays, Muslims flock to the mosque on Fridays. But fewer people come for the prayers during the week, and I wanted to pray in a non-combative environment where it was just about prayer and peace – something that had gone out the window with the Battle of the Shower Curtain.

As I walked in, the first thing I noticed was that the shower curtain was gone. I was elated. The Saudi imam must have backed down. Just then a man with a red-hued beard walked towards me.

'Excuse me, sister, but this is the men's prayer room,' said Red Beard. 'Only men are allowed to pray in here.' He pointed to a large and elaborate sign: MEN'S PRAYER ROOM. It might as well have said NO GIRLS ALLOWED.

'But this mosque is for women too,' I replied, frustrated.

'Of course it is, and now you have your own special room.' Red Beard directed me to the office behind the main prayer hall. The door now read WOMEN'S PRAYER ROOM, and the space had been renovated so that there was a two-way mirror, the kind used in police interrogations, in place of the previous built-in bookshelves.

'Look,' said Red Beard. 'You can look out at the men but they can't see you.'

We both stood in the women's room, looking out through the mirror at the men praying on the other side. The curtain had been bad, but at least we were in the same room. This interrogation-style mirror made me feel like I was being buried somewhere deep inside the mosque so my presence could be erased. I couldn't do it.

'I don't really care if the men can see me,' I said. 'I'm just here to pray.'

A man with a long black beard came up on the other side of the window and looked at me.

'I think he can see me,' I told Red Beard.

'No, that's not possible,' he said. Black Beard pulled out a comb and started to fix his hair.

'Why's he combing his hair?' I asked.

Red Beard was very happy. 'See, he doesn't see you at all – he sees himself in a mirror. It works perfectly. Now you have your own separate but equal space.'

'Separate but *un*equal space,' I corrected.

Black Beard pulled out a nail clipper and started trimming his nose hairs. Apparently, this was too much for Red Beard. I followed him out of the women's room and back into the main prayer hall. Red Beard told Black Beard that women could see him.

'I used to use the bathroom in that office to take care of my grooming needs,' Black Beard complained.

'There's another washroom in the basement,' Red Beard told him. 'Use that one.'

'The basement is far away. Besides, there aren't any women praying in that room. Can't I use it?'

'Sure, knock yourself out,' I said. 'I'm not praying in there.'

'But, dear sister, we've given you your very own room,' said Red Beard. 'Why don't you want to use it?'

'During the time of the Prophet, if a woman felt that some-one was impinging on her rights, she would speak up and complain – because she was in the same room with no barrier in front of her,' I said. 'How are we going to do that now?'

'Just send a note,' said Red Beard.

I arched an eyebrow at him. There was no way I was buying what he was selling. Women were being treated like truant children, punished for being born female. But he didn't give up.

'We made it nice for you. We even put in a new carpet, look.' He beckoned me back into the room. Black Beard followed us and made a beeline for the washroom.

'It is pretty,' I said, flicking on the lights to stare at the pink shag. But Red Beard looked upset. I thought it was the sound of Black Beard gargling, but Red Beard was staring at the mirror.

'What's wrong?' I asked. 'Is it the wrong shade of pink?'

'I can't see through the glass,' said Red Beard, perplexed, as the view of the main prayer hall was gradually replaced by a reflection of the room we were in. With the lights on inside, the women's room was brighter than the men's room during sunset, which resulted in the two-way mirror reversing direction.

'I have spinach in my teeth,' I said, examining my face.

'This is not going to work,' said Red Beard. 'The men can see in.'

'I know, right,' I said, happy that he was coming to his senses.

'Let's turn out the lights.' He flipped the switch and the room became pitch black. 'We'll add a curtain to the window, so at night you can leave the lights on.'

'But then we can't see the prayer leader,' I complained.

'But you can hear the prayer leader. The speakers in here are excellent.'

Black Beard came out of the washroom, tripped on the carpet and fell at our feet.

'Why are the lights out?' he exclaimed.

'Why are you in the women's prayer room?' said Red Beard.

'Because I had to use the washroom,' said Black Beard.

The three of us stood there in the dark.

'Well, this is awkward,' said Red Beard.

'And it's very dark,' said Black Beard. The call to prayer started and the three of us trooped out and prayed in the main/men's/disputed prayer hall. I went home.

'How was the mosque?' asked Sami as he unloaded the dishwasher.

'It gets weirder every time I go,' I replied.

The problem as I saw it was that Muslims themselves saw barriers in front of women as something mandated by religion. They needed to be educated about their own faith.

'Is this Zarqa Nawaz?' asked Joe McDonald, a producer for the National Film Board. He wanted to know if I'd like to submit a proposal for a documentary. 'Is there a topic you're passionate about?' he asked.

Why yes, there is.

I had left my journalism roots behind, but there was no time like the present to resurrect them for a good cause.

I threw myself into the research. I wanted to figure out how tradition had become mistaken for theology. My initial proposal was seething, but somehow the NFB accepted it – with the caveat that I not be quite so hard on my community.

'Just remember that there are women who prefer the privacy of a separate area,' Sami cautioned me. 'You can't discount their feelings.' His sensible-ness was getting annoying, but he was right, I did want to be fair to women who were in favour of a segregated space. So I decided to interview my mother, who represented more conservative Muslim views. I called her.

'Yes, I'm coming to Toronto for work again.'

'Are you bringing the children?' she asked.

'No, they're all in school,' I said, thinking she'd be relieved. 'I want to interview you for a documentary I'm making about barriers in mosques.'

'But the children need their mother at home,' said my mother.

'In our home, they probably need their father more.'

I took my mother and the camera crew to her favourite mosque in Toronto. The women prayed behind the men, with only a knee-high Plexiglas barrier between them. Men and women could easily see each other as they milled about in the cavernous prayer hall. There was a crying room at one end for women with babies.

'I pray here five times a day,' said my mother. 'I enjoy coming here.'

'Was there a barrier in your mosque in Pakistan?'

'We never went to the mosque,' she said. 'It was for men only. I only started going to the mosque when I came to Canada.'

Mosques in some Muslim countries are like pit stops for men who need to do their daily prayers while on the run. Mosques in North America are like Muslim community centres, where there is accommodation for everyone.

'Do you feel a little odd coming to a mosque without a physical barrier between the men and women?'

'I heard a male scholar say that there were no barriers during the time of the Prophet. So praying like this is allowed,' said my mother.

'So if scholars tell you it's OK, then you're fine with it?' I asked.

'Real scholars, not people like you with your modern ideas.'

Clearly I needed to bring in some heavy hitters. I called my contact at the NFB, but there just wasn't the budget to fly a camera crew and me to the Middle East. I was adding up my air miles when my mother suggested that we attend a new Islamic conference in Toronto called 'Reviving the Islamic Spirit'. I checked the speakers – it was the perfect list of scholars and they all looked the part. There would be enough beards and robes at this conference for a casting call for *The Ten Commandments*. It was a sign from God.

'Don't drag God into this,' my mother said.

While my mother sat in the lecture hall, I managed to convince one of the harried organizers to give me a room in the conference centre, where I set up my camera crew. As each speaker left the main hall, I pounced.

'Excuse me, I'm making a documentary about female segregation in the mosque, and I wondered if you would be willing to comment on camera?' I asked one serious-looking scholar.

'This problem again,' he said, a little annoyed. This surprised me.

'You're familiar with it?' I asked.

'Too much,' he said wearily. 'Where are the cameras?'

To my wonderment, the scholars were more than willing to speak to me.

'It's a cultural problem,' said one, 'not a religious one. There's no religious requirement for barriers. It came about when Islam spread and started incorporating the traditions of cultures where segregation was the norm. Both women and men have to grow used to the idea of worshipping without barriers in the same space. But until then, mosques with either strong leadership or a congregation that is forceful about equality will be the ones without barriers.'

I was a little taken aback by his forwardness. It gave me a warm, fuzzy feeling that this senior cleric was so pro-women.

Mosques without any barriers between men and women were rare, but the Aurora Mosque in Chicago was one of them. I visited it. A husband-and-wife team had built it without even a symbolic partition like the knee-high Plexiglas at my mother's mosque.

'We knew right away that building with others would mean compromise,' the man told me. 'So we decided to do it on our own terms and avoid conflict. And since I had the money, why not?'

The mosque was beautiful and airy, with peach carpets and a large iron chandelier hanging in the prayer area. I felt that I could relax and just listen to the sermon while the men respectfully shuffled past me. But I noticed that some of the women still sat right at the back and tried to hide behind the pillars.

'It's a start,' said the man. 'There are people who complain and ask for a barrier, but we tell them that they'll have to get used to praying without it.'

After months spent travelling and shooting over 150 hours of footage, and another several months editing it all together, the documentary was finally done. I felt ebullient. I knew it couldn't change the Muslim community, but if it was just a tiny bit influential, all the time would have been worth it.

Me and the Mosque premiered at the Montreal World Film Festival. Then it screened on Vision TV and finally on CBC Television.

Making a documentary that was critical of the community didn't made me popular. Friends thought my timing was terrible and that I was handing ammunition to the 'Muslims are sexist' publicity machine. They felt we should sort out our issues in private. But I felt that the outside world would judge us less harshly if it saw that we too were struggling with gender equality. I held my breath as my community reacted.

'I like it,' said Blue Scarf, a conservative Muslim woman.

'Are you going to pray in the main hall?' I asked hopefully.

'No, I like it here,' she said. 'It's more private.'

'Not bad,' said Red Beard. 'I was very impressed that you got those scholars to talk to you.'

'So now you understand my mania for wanting to pray in the main prayer hall?'

'Yes, but I still think it's better for men and women to be separate.'

The board of the mosque convened a meeting to discuss the ongoing issue of women's prayer space and decided to allow women to pray wherever they chose. But while making a decision like that was easy, getting the congregation to accept it was not. The board removed the signs that indicated that the main hall was the men's. But new ones kept going up. The Battle of the Shower Curtain was replaced by the Battle of the Signs.

One day a young man from Saudi Arabia approached me.

'I watched your documentary,' he said. 'And I have something to say.'

'You hated it,' I said, assuming that being from Saudi Arabia would automatically put him on one side.

'No, I was the one who made the original signs,' he said.

'The ones that said "Women's Prayer Room", "Men's Prayer Room"?'

'When I saw my signs in your documentary, I was a little shocked. I had no idea they were making you feel excluded. I'm sorry.'

'They were very pretty signs,' I said, feeling guilty for judging him. I looked sadly at the ugly computer-generated ones.

'Thank you. I wanted the women to feel special.'

I don't want to feel special, I thought. I just want to feel normal and be able to pray where I want without hostile glares from men who feel I don't belong there.

Black Beard approached me as I walked into the main prayer hall.

'Good film,' he said. 'I wish the women would pray here again.'

'Because you believe in equality?'

'Because I want to get our bathroom back.'

It was a start.

Little Mosque in the City

'Don't leave the prayer hall,' said Sami on the phone. I could hear the stress in his voice. Something had gone wrong after Friday prayers. Right after the sermon ended, shouting erupted in the main prayer hall. I looked through the one-way glass and saw agitated men surrounding Sami. It was the first time in my life I was glad to be praying in the women's section.

'It's your *Little Mosque on the Prairie*,' said one of my friends. 'Some of the men are angry. They believe the show makes fun of Islam.'

I felt a sense of horrible dread as I sank down on the carpet and put my head on my knees. My new TV show, *Little Mosque on the Prairie*, had just starting airing on CBC Television. I called Sami on his cellphone.

'What are the men saying?' I asked, frightened.

'They want me to divorce you. They keep yelling, "Shame, shame." Just stay where you are until they leave. We're going to be fine.'

I had thought Muslims would be thrilled with a TV depiction of our community that didn't feature the usual stereotypes of gun-toting terrorists. But now I was holed up in a mosque, waiting for a mob to leave. I started crying, mostly out of disappointment and anger.

'Don't cry,' said my friend. 'You haven't done anything wrong.'

Hadn't I?

After writing and directing a few short films, I had spent a few years writing a screenplay for a feature film about a Muslim actor who is offered a role as a terrorist about to hijack a plane. He desperately needs the money to pay for an engagement ring for his fiancée. Finally, I landed a pitch meeting with a prominent producer.

'This is the single worst pitch I've heard in my entire career,' he told me.

'But it's a very funny script,' I protested.

'Do you even remember 9/11?'

'Of course.'

'Then you can't be serious about this screenplay,' said the producer, exasperated. 'You have written the one script that is not producible in the seeing world. You can't make a comedy about a Muslim hijacking a plane!'

'But it's been five years since 9/11, and no one actually hijacks anything,' I argued. 'He's an *actor*, not a terrorist.'

'No one will ever be able to make a comedy about hijacking a plane, ever, EVER,' he said. 'You are a very enthusiastic writer, but this is not happening. Do you hear me?'

'What about the film *The Producers*?' I countered. 'The play within the film is called *Springtime for Hitler*. And that film was so popular it became a Broadway play.'

'You can't be serious,' he said. 'That film was made decades after World War Two and was considered controversial and in poor taste then. Maybe in a hundred years this movie could be made, but by then you and I will both be dead.'

I went home and sulked. I knew I was crazy for even pitching it, but I had trouble giving up the dream.

'Sami, I came up with this idea long before 9/11 and now I can't make it.'

'Yes, that's the *real* tragedy of 9/11,' said Sami sarcastically.

'My career is over. I'll never be able to work again,' I said dramatically.

'Or you could just write another comedy,' he said. 'Writers are called writers for a reason. They write.'

Then the National Film Board of Canada asked me to attend the Banff World Television Festival in Alberta: it wanted to show off its documentary makers.

'What do writers do at this festival?' I asked my friend Anita.

She said, 'They pitch television series,' and sent me some templates.

I was making my doc *Me and the Mosque* at the time, so fitting Islam into the modern world was uppermost in my mind. I started to wonder how the dynamics of a mosque would change if an imam was from Canada and supportive of women. So I wrote a film treatment about a young hot-shot Muslim lawyer in Toronto who decides his life in corporate law is sucking his soul dry. Wanting to do something more spiritually fulfilling with his life, he happens to read a 'wanted' ad for an imam job in a tiny, broken-down mosque in Saskatchewan. He takes the job, thinking of it as a fresh start in life.

I set up pitch meetings with various producers in Banff.

'I wrote a screenplay about a Muslim actor who gets a role hijacking a plane—'

'Pass,' said the producer, cutting me off. 'We were told you had a TV series to pitch.'

. I pulled out my treatment about the young man who becomes an imam. I had put the mosque in a church because the mosque I had attended as a child was a former church, and the two structures had merged in my consciousness. Stained glass and choir balconies were more Muslim than Christian to me. As I pitched the series, a surprising thing happened. People got excited.

'This is an amazing idea,' said the producer from WestWind Pictures.

'You're not talking about the hijacking screenplay, are you?' I said.

'No, that's a terrible idea. Please stop talking about it.'

A few months later, I heard that Anton Leo, the head of comedy for CBC Television, was soliciting pitches from across the country. Michael Snook from WestWind Pictures and I went to the CBC offices in Regina to meet him. After some small-talk, Anton sat back and said, 'All right, pitch me.'

I stared at him blankly. Michael cleared his throat and looked at me. Clearly everyone was expecting me to speak.

'OK, there's a Muslim actor who gets a role as a hijacker—'

'Not that pitch,' said Michael. I felt a kick under the table. 'She has it all written here,' he said, pushing the treatment forward.

'Right,' I replied, wishing that I had reread the pitch documents I had written six months earlier. 'The new imam is different from what the Muslim community would normally expect an imam to look like: he's clean-shaven, wears suits . . . '

'So this is a classic fish-out-of-water story?' Anton asked.

'I'm pretty sure there are no fish in this pitch,' I said, confused.

'Ha ha, she's so funny,' replied a nervous Michael. 'But yes, it's a classic fish-out-of-water story. The imam is from Toronto and goes to live in a rural town in Saskatchewan. Zarqa's actually from Toronto herself, and it's slightly autobiographical.'

We left the room.

'It wasn't a great pitch, was it?' I asked.

'Well, it wasn't stellar, but I think we're going into development,' Michael said.

'Really?'

'Yes, it's a great concept that even you can't screw up.'

After three months, all seven episodes of *Little Mosque* were done. The CBC asked me to be in Toronto when the show premiered, so I could continue the publicity. I watched the first episode with my parents.

'What did you think?' I asked my mother, who sat with me, knitting a sweater.

'I think you should be home with your children,' she said.

'No, I mean the show,' I said. 'What do you think about the show?'

'I thought the hijabs were very pretty,' she said. 'Where did you get them?'

The phone rang a few hours later. It was a reporter.

'The ratings came in for the first episode,' he said.

I had been waiting for this. A lot of Canadian shows fail because, unlike American broadcasters, our broadcasters don't have million-dollar advertising budgets. But this time, American media's obsession with our show meant we were getting the press attention we needed.

'What were they?'

'Two point one million!' he said.

'It's very good,' said the reporter. '*Little Mosque* has breathed new life into the network. Think of it this way, it's as if PBS had discovered *CSI*.'

'I don't think anyone saw this coming,' I said.

'A hit religious comedy show about Muslims worshipping in a broken-down mosque, within a broken-down church, living in a tiny town in the Canadian Midwest?' said the reporter. 'I can guarantee you, no one saw that coming.'

'Thanks,' I said, not sure if he was complimenting me.

I flew home to Saskatchewan. Zayn, now six, was waiting for me at the door.

'I don't like it when you leave,' he said, hugging me.

'He's fine,' said Sami. 'But he likes to manipulate you.'

'I'm not fine,' said Zayn. 'I cry in school.'

'See,' said Sami. 'Don't let him make you feel guilty.'

Sami picked Zayn up and took him to bed while I grabbed the newspaper. I was interested in the media reaction to the show. I read Margaret Wente, one of my favourite columnists at the *Globe and Mail*. She wasn't excited.

'If there's an imam on earth who resembles this one, I will convert to Islam, don the veil, and catch the next plane to Mecca.'

I was a little shocked that Margaret didn't believe that among the billion Muslims on earth there might not be a few good-looking imams. I contemplated sending a picture of Sami to her, but then again, having Margaret in the mosque would be a little unnerving.

But she wasn't the only naysayer. Every time I met a Muslim that week, they objected to something they saw in the show.

'We want a show that projects us as perfect Muslims,' said White Scarf.

'That's called propaganda,' I said. 'And it's limited to puppet shows and children's programming.'

'Do you really think that Muslim women don't have to cover themselves in front of gay men?' asked Brown Turban.

'It's a question worth asking,' I said.

'Only if you want to ask it in hell,' said Brown Turban.

'You showed menstrual blood on TV,' said Black Scarf. 'I had to cover my child's eyes.'

'But Islam is very open about menstruation,' I said. 'Why are Muslims squeamish about things that God and his Prophet talked about with sensitivity?'

'Kissing a man in public?' said Pink Scarf, outraged. 'Pinching a man's butt in the mosque? These are not Islamic behaviours.'

'But they're married,' I countered.

Growing up as a Canadian Muslim meant that I had absorbed a more relaxed attitude about intimacy. Sami and I kissed and cuddled in front of our kids, who viewed it as gross but loving behaviour. But neither my parents nor Sami's showed physical affection in front of us. They came from a culture that was more reserved. They didn't even use their first names with each other because it was considered too intimate. The characters on *Little Mosque* behaved like I do, which, ironically, was closer to the behaviour of the early Muslim community than the one that existed around me now. Week after week, people at my mosque grew more agitated. They were acting as if I had just made *Porn on the Prairie*. It was becoming clear that I lived in a conservative immigrant community who felt that poking fun at Muslims was tantamount to making fun of Islam. They couldn't distinguish between the two.

The swell of anger and indignation had come to a head at

that fateful Friday prayer. People wanted my head on a platter, and I cowered in the back of the women's section, wondering how my life had come to this sorry state.

When the crowd eventually dissipated, Sami and I went home. He was furious that people had behaved in this manner. I was hoping the whole thing would just disappear, but a few days later the Islamic Association of Saskatchewan was presented with a petition to have me removed from the mosque. Sami was the secretary of the board at the time. He excused himself during the meetings where I was the topic of discussion. The board ruled that they couldn't control how a member of the community behaved, but the petitioners persisted.

'What do you want us to do?' said a member of the board sarcastically. 'Should we burn her house down?' I wondered if that's what would have happened if I lived anywhere else in the world. But I lived in Regina, where I was safe to poke affectionate fun at Muslims. I decided to put the board out of its misery by resigning from the Islamic Association of Saskatchewan. They returned my $25 membership fee.

'I really thought Muslims would love this show,' I said that evening. I was alone with Sami, scrolling through blogs. I felt a little broken, discouraged and despondent. It was difficult to belong to a community that treated me like an outcast.

'Look, this is the first television show about a mosque-based Muslim community in North America, possibly the world,' said Sami. 'And you tipped some sacred cows.' He took the computer away from me.

'I didn't mean to tip them. I just wanted to show them some new pastures,' I said, trying to sort out the last few confusing days.

'Write the show you want,' he said. 'Trust me, they'll move

on to something else. One day the same people who hate *Little Mosque* might end up loving it.'

I doubted it. Conservative Muslims are a tough nut to crack. I felt crushed under the weight of their collective judgement. I took Sami's advice and stopped reading Internet comments, but it would be a while before I could go to the mosque again. The mosque had once been a place of repose, but now it was a place with a lot of bad memories.

'I'm not sure I want to be around Muslims right now.'

It turned out that I didn't have to see much of my community after all. I got a call from Michael Snook.

'Zarqa, the CBC's decided to green-light the series. They've ordered twenty episodes,' he said.

'That's great news,' I said, my disappointment washing away. I was officially excited again. 'And did they make a decision about where to shoot the show?'

'Toronto,' said Michael. 'I know that's disappointing for you, but CBC feels it's best. We'll need you back here.'

'For how long?'

'Six months.'

We had shot the first two episodes of *Little Mosque* in Regina, using my kitchen for some of the family scenes. After an exhausting two years of travelling for *Me and the Mosque*, it had been a relief to be able to come home to Sami and the kids every night. The remaining five episodes had been shot in Toronto, which took me away for three months. Now, with Michael and me being the only members of the team living in Saskatchewan, the CBC executives, who were known for wanting to be closely involved in all aspects of a show's creation, wanted the show to be shot in Toronto, where they could continue to nurture it.

'Sami, I'm going to tell Anton I can't do it,' I said, looking at Zayn colouring at the dining-room table.

'Why would you do that?'

'Because of the kids,' I said. 'What will happen to them?'

'Nothing will happen to them,' said Sami. 'They have their father.'

Zayn looked up. 'Is Mama going again?' He burst into tears.

'Look what's happening to him,' I said, perturbed. 'He's crying.'

'It's called emotional manipulation.'

'It's working. Maybe the writers could do it without me?'

'A bunch of white writers who've never darkened the door of a mosque can't suddenly be expected to make a comedy about mosque life. Plus this is the biggest thing that's happened in your career.'

I had worked so hard to make it as a writer, and now the success felt bittersweet. Somehow I figured my career and family would always be in tandem. But with the kids no longer portable, I'd have to leave them all behind. I flew to Toronto and, to my mother's great annoyance, moved into a rented condo. I couldn't live with her. I already felt guilty about leaving my family and she would just add to my turmoil.

On set, the designer had built the interior of the mosque, just as I'd asked, complete with colourful carpets, five tacky wall clocks and a half-barrier between the men and the women – I had to be accurate, after all. It miraculously faced north-east, so on my first day I decided to do my prayers there. It was a piece of home, but unlike home, it was calm and restful. I was a congregation of one. That space became my sanctuary – my little mosque in the city.

*

Six tumultuous seasons later, *Little Mosque on the Prairie* ended its run. Relaxing, I was watching a new series entitled *Citizen Khan*, a hilarious and irreverent BBC sitcom about the British Muslim community.

I scrolled down to the comments section on the BBC website and read the predictable rants from outraged Muslims, until I came to one that stopped me.

'This is no *Little Mosque on the Prairie*. Now *that* was a show that was respectful to everyone.'

Jinn – a Muslim Thing

I ran back from the gas station store to the pumps, where Sami was filling up the minivan.

'I need you to come with me while I pee,' I told him.

'Why, did you forget how?' he said, startled. 'It's like riding a bike, you can't forget.'

I thrust out a key attached by a chain to a plank of wood. My hand was actually shaking. 'The washroom isn't inside the gas station. The owner told me to walk a few metres into the forest, where they built the outhouse.'

'Are you worried about getting lost?' he asked. 'I can see it from here.'

'Just hold my hand. Why is it so hard to be a good husband?' I was frustrated by his thick-headedness.

'As a good husband I hold your hand in times of stress, which this is not.' He got back into the minivan and started the engine. 'Let's go.'

'No, I have to pee!' I cried.

He took the key out of the ignition. 'So go!'

'What kind of gas station has an *outhouse*?' I wailed, and got into the passenger seat so he could better see my panic. He needed to understand that this was deathly important.

'This kind,' says Sami. He wasn't taking my fears of imminent doom seriously. 'Why are you freaking out about this? Wait, what movie were you watching as we pulled in? Did it by chance involve someone being possessed?'

'Um. No, it was the story of a nice girl named Emily Rose. Kind of like an *Anne of Green Gables* thing? But it wigged me out.' I am the worst liar. 'So I need you to come with me.'

We were on our way home from a family holiday in Panorama, Alberta, and I had foolishly brought along a DVD of *The Exorcism of Emily Rose*. Sami discouraged me from watching movies involving possession, because I always became a little unhinged afterwards and he had to deal with the fall-out. So I'd had to sneak *Emily Rose* into my laptop, watching it surreptitiously while he was watching the road. I mean, really, no one does exorcism better than the Catholics.

'What does "possessed" mean, Abbu?' Zayn asked Sami from the back.

'It means when they take something back because you can't pay for it,' said Inaya.

'Did Abbu forget to pay for Mama?' he asked.

'No, you're all silly,' said Maysa, displaying all the wisdom of a twelve-year-old. 'Being possessed means having an ability you never had before, right, Abbu,' turning to her father, 'like speaking French?'

'Or becoming invisible,' said Inaya, mesmerized. 'Is Mama going to disappear?'

'Only if I leave without her,' replied Sami. 'Which I'm seriously thinking about. Why did you bring that movie? You know how crazy you get.'

Herein lies the crux of my problem. Superman's superpower is his incredible strength, and mine is the ability to watch horror movies without flinching or suffering nightmares. Even the *Saw* movies were fine until they got a little tedious: yet another guy waking up in the basement with some sort of meat grinder attached to his testicles, ready to pulverize his twig and berries if he didn't answer some question properly. Yawn. But possession is my kryptonite.

Muslims don't believe in ghosts or in zombie viruses that allow you to go on undead forever, eating the living for nourishment (with the exception of Hugh Hefner, whom we disapprove of). Once you're put into the ground, you're never coming back to haunt anyone. If you didn't have a chance to say goodbye properly, want to tell the police who murdered you, or need to pass on an urgent secret, it's too late. A Muslim never has the chance to scrawl the words 'A spoonful of grape jelly in the meat sauce was my secret to the lasagne' on a steamed mirror after someone's shower. If Patrick Swayze's character had been Muslim, *Ghost* would have been over in five minutes.

According to Islam, you get one shot at this life, and once your soul departs, it's a one-way ticket straight into the light, no reminders about dry-cleaning for the living. Muslims believe only white people coming out of comas see the white light. I don't know what Muslims see after they come out of comas – probably bickering relatives. So horror movies have no effect on me at all. No nightmares or lingering worries. Unless they involve possession. Then I must watch with sick fascination until the end. But watching those movies comes at a price.

'I could have a picnic in a graveyard,' I said. 'That's how brave I am.'

'So prove it to me by going to the outhouse,' replied Sami drily. 'I'd really like to leave soon.'

I stared him down. 'I could get possessed by a jinn,' I hissed.

'And I could get eaten by a dingo,' Sami said.

'What's a jinn?' asked Zayn.

Sami looked at me.

'I'll take this,' I replied. 'OK, so you know how Muslims believe that humans are made from clay, and angels are made from light?'

'Yep,' said Zayn.

'We also believe in a third creation. They're called jinn and they're made from smokeless fire.'

'Are jinn ghosts?' asked Zayn.

'No, but they're invisible to the human eye, like God and Wi-Fi.'

'This is not the way kids should be taught about religion,' said Sami with apprehension.

'Relax,' I replied. 'Think of it as a real-world lesson.'

'Except that it's not very real,' he grumbled.

'But what's a jinn?' asked Zayn.

'They're kind of like people – they have free will, marry, have kids, follow different religions – but they're invisible and live in areas that aren't inhabited by humans. Outhouses in a forest are a magnet for jinn.'

I knew that sounded crazy but that's what I believed.

'So that's why Mama can't pee outside,' said Maysa.

'Apparently,' said Sami. 'But she's made jinn into monsters in her mind.' Sami believed that jinn were more like bad subconscious inclinations, like a devil on one of your shoulders, opposing the angel on the other. But I believed that sometimes the world of jinn and humans intersected. What to me was an outhouse could be a three-bedroom ranch for a jinn. And then it would take me for an intruder, get mad and possess me in retaliation, and I'd become just like Emily Rose.

'Can jinn watch her while she pees?' asked Zayn.

'No one watches you while you pee,' said Sami.

'I watch Rashad sometimes,' said Zayn.

'Abbu!' yelled Rashad.

'No one watches you as long as you lock the door.' Sami looked at Zayn. 'Stop watching your brother.'

'How much longer before we get home?' I asked.

'Really, you're going to wait that long?'

'Don't you remember the stories growing up? They can change into the shape of a human except for one part, like a hairy paw, which stays in their true animal form.'

'Mama's pretty hairy,' said Zayn.

'Yeah, she is,' said Inaya, looking at me with curiosity. 'Can you become invisible?'

'My friend Anila told me that jinn can make themselves look human when it's convenient for them,' said Maysa. 'And that some of them are Muslim.'

'Sometimes Mama just disappears when it's story time,' said Rashad. 'Like she became invisible.'

The kids looked at me suspiciously.

'I'm not a jinn,' I yelled, looking at Sami for support.

'You started this,' he said unsympathetically.

'Jinn eat poo and live in forests, which I do not do,' I said to Sami.

'Yuck,' said Maysa.

'Or do they eat bones? What did you learn, poo or bones?'

Sami didn't have the decency to answer me. He started the engine. But I didn't let it deter me.

'What were the rules again? Don't sit on them or pour hot water on them. But what I don't get is, if you can't see them, how are you supposed to not step on them and make them mad enough to possess you?' I said. 'It's a huge dilemma.'

'I'm sure for you it is,' he said.

'Make fun of me all you want, but some people believe that they can mate with humans. Maybe I'm the outhouse jinn's type.'

'No one is anyone's type on the toilet,' responded Sami.

'What if they wanted to eat my poo, mate with me and then possess me?'

Sami refused to answer. I couldn't understand why he wasn't taking me seriously. I opened the door and got out cautiously. I returned moments later.

'That was quick,' said Sami.

'I was just returning the key,' I said glumly. 'Let's just go home as fast as possible.'

Sami put the minivan into drive and we merged on to the highway, leaving my outhouse of doom behind. I felt every bump and jolt for the next two hours.

Catholics believe that demons can possess bodies, and some Muslims, like me, believe that jinn can do the same thing. But Catholics demand that a person be put through a rigorous psychiatric evaluation to rule out mental illness before jumping to the possession diagnosis. Sami, who is a psychiatrist, must have come across the occasional possessed person.

'You're sure none of your patients ever rotated their heads 180 degrees?' I asked.

'Nope.'

'Anyone ever levitate on the Psych Unit?'

'Nope.'

'So you never whispered the last three chapters from the Qur'an to miraculously cure a patient?' Muslims believe reciting those three chapters is one way to repel a jinn.

'Nope.'

'People go crazy for all sorts of reasons, and possession could be one of them,' I said.

But Sami believed all diseases of the mind – schizophrenia, depression, bipolar disorder – were caused by chemical imbalances and could be treated by modern medicine. How he still called himself a Muslim was beyond me. I should have asked him about his views on possession before I married him, but now it was too late. I had no one to hold my hand in an outhouse and now my bladder felt like it was about to have an aneurysm.

By the time we pulled up to the house, it was 2 a.m.

'I'll get the luggage, you get the kids,' said Sami as I flew out of the van and hurtled towards the bathroom, which was mercifully free from supernatural beings. As I nearly cried from relief, I decided Sami was right. No more possession movies.

I could hear the kids banging around the house, getting ready to sleep.

'I need to cuddle with you in bed,' I told Sami.

'Fine. But you don't get to complain you can't sleep because of my snoring,' he said. When his snoring got too loud I often moved to another room or had him sleep in the basement. But tonight I didn't feel like being alone. I popped in earplugs to block out the snoring and hung on to Sami for dear life as I finally fell asleep. I dreamed about adult diapers chasing demons.

Then I woke, sensing a presence hovering above my body. It couldn't be. I was too frightened to open my eyes, since I knew what this meant: I was about to be possessed. A jinn must have decided I was his type after all and followed me home from the gas station, even though I'd never made it to the outhouse. So this is how it starts. I wondered if Sami would even notice that I was gone, in spirit if not body. It was getting closer and closer, and I could feel its hot breath on my face. Finally I couldn't take it any more and opened my eyes.

It was Zayn. A distinctly terrified and blue-looking Zayn.

'You left me in the van,' he said with chattering teeth.

Sami woke up. 'What's going on?' he said, rubbing his eyes.

'Mama forgot me in the van, and I woke up when my toes got too cold.' Zayn squeezed in between the two of us. I rubbed his toes and fingers while trying to avoid Sami's gaze. The prairies got chilly at night during the fall.

'You didn't check to see if all the kids were out of the van?' he asked.

'I could hear them running around the house,' I stammered. 'I just assumed they were all out. I'm so sorry, Zayn.' I felt horrible. The kids weren't babies any more and were capable of getting out of the car on their own, but still I felt like I had failed my child.

'Were you scared?' Sami asked him.

'It was so dark. I got out really slowly and walked up the garage stairs.' He stopped shivering from the cold. 'And I tried really hard not to think about jinn trying to eat me.'

'They don't eat you,' I started, but then decided this wasn't the time to sort out the niceties of possession. 'I'm really sorry.' I smoothed his hair. 'I promise never to watch a movie about possession again.'

'And you promise to pee in an outhouse toilet if the need calls for it?' asked Sami.

That is a terrible thing to ask of someone, I thought.

'Fine,' I said, 'but if I get possessed, you'll be sorry.'

'How would we know?' asked Zayn.

'I don't know,' I said. 'I'd probably say crazy things and do crazy things, and you wouldn't really be able to understand me. I wouldn't be that rational.'

Zayn and Sami looked at each other.

'I think we'd all manage,' said Sami, rolling over. His snoring started again.

As I lay there watching the two of them sleep, I realized that I'd have to get my fears under control. Or else my family might stage an intervention. Or, worse, let me get possessed, hoping for an improvement. But right now, I needed to pee.

I looked at the bathroom. It was dark. I looked at the clock. It was only three hours until dawn. I could wait.

Eid Dinner

'What day is Eid this year?' I asked Sami.

'Google it,' he replied.

'Christians are lucky,' I said resentfully. 'They know when Christmas is every year.'

Even Scientologists know when to turn off the E-meter and take a break, but Muslims? It's complicated. We still follow the lunar calendar, instead of the regular Gregorian calendar, to calculate the dates for our celebrations. And that means Eid al-Fitr, the celebration at the end of Ramadan, moves up by about eleven days every year. The Jews also follow the lunar calendar, but make adjustments by adding a leap month every few years to keep the dates roughly the same. But for Muslims, it takes thirty-five years for a holiday to fall on the same date again in the regular calendar. This means that Muslims will never pull it together. Or *this* Muslim won't. I have trouble remembering my kids' birthdays, and those dates don't wander nearly as much.

'Uh oh, I booked a laser hair-removal session for that day,' I told Sami when I looked up the date.

'Mama's not coming with us for Eid prayers?' asked Zayn fretfully.

'She's cancelling her appointment,' Sami told him. 'Didn't you check the date for Eid before you booked that?'

'Eid is like finding a needle in a moving haystack,' I said. 'Who checks the date for Eid before they book things?'

'I do,' he said. 'I schedule three days off for both Eids to cover the range of possibilities three years in advance so I don't have any conflicts.'

Did I mention that there's a second Eid – Eid al-Adha – with the same wandering-date problem? Eid al-Adha celebrates the almost-sacrifice of Abraham's son, who was saved when God decreed a ram (or goat, depending on who you talk to) be sacrificed instead. We like to keep things interesting.

'Wow, Abbu really cares about us,' said Zayn.

And Abbu's a bit of a freak, I thought, but I was more annoyed at the insinuation that I was a substandard mother.

'Family always comes first,' said Sami.

And then the words came out of my mouth before I could stop them.

'This year, I'll cook the big Eid dinner for everyone,' I told Zayn. 'We'll invite all of your aunts and uncles and cousins to our house.'

Sami put down the newspaper. He looked worried. I felt worried. I could barely cook dinner for our family, and this was a feast for over thirty people. But then, suddenly, I was calm. Sami's mother loved cooking the big Eid dinner. And she was good at it. She'd refuse my offer and I could save face while still looking like a good wife and mother. It was perfect.

'Where's this coming from?' Sami asked.

'From my heart, where else would it come from?'

'That's awesome! Can I help?' asked Zayn.

'Sure, you can be my sous-chef,' I replied.

'But I get to chop vegetables with a real knife?' he asked.

'Wait, my mother cooks that dinner,' said Sami. 'It's tradition. Maybe you could put up the streamers and balloons or something?'

'Well, it's time to change the tradition. Your mother's getting older, and somebody around here has to look out for her. After all, family comes *first*.' I was totally winning this. Best mother ever.

'When it comes to dinner, food comes first. And my mother actually knows how to cook.'

'I can cook,' I said.

Sami blinked. There was a look of mild panic on his face. 'Eid is special. And my mom makes amazing food that day.'

'I can make amazing food too.'

Sami, Maysa and Zayn all looked at each other. I'd gone too far. I needed to retreat to defend my position or else they'd never believe me.

'I can *learn* to cook amazing food. Not knowing how to be a brilliant cook isn't a permanent thing, like not having an eye or something,' I said as I put on my shoes. 'I did master the Rice Krispie square.'

'Where are you going?' asked Sami, looking concerned.

'To talk about my menu with your mother,' I replied and walked next door.

My mother-in-law listened carefully to my 'plan'. I laid it all out, and then awaited her refusal. I'd offer to decorate. I had a great idea for a Kaaba made out of Rice Krispie squares as a centrepiece.

She sat down, smoothed her grey hair and regarded me for a few moments. She was preparing to let me down easy.

'I *am* getting tired,' she said. 'It would be nice to have some-one else take over.'

'Oh, of course, I wouldn't want to hurt— Wait, *what*?' I stuttered.

'You should cook what you know. This is not the time to experiment,' she said solemnly. I could barely hear her over the buzzing of panic in my ears. This was terrible. I had a sudden vision of forty people picking dubiously at their burnt food, whispering, 'She ruined Eid' to each other while eyeing me distastefully, and then making a pact to meet at Burger King. I needed to focus.

'Zarqa, you're very good at making curry. I think for your first Eid dinner you should stick to that.' She was right. If everything I made was a variation of curry, maybe I could do this. Maybe I could create a tradition of my own. Both my mother and my mother-in-law were beloved for their elaborate feasts. Why couldn't I be beloved in the same way?

While she talked to me about logistics and strategies, I became distracted by a cooking show on TV behind her. Two women were analysing how to make a healthy version of butter chicken, the famous Indian dish. It was technically a curry but different enough to become my new famous signature dish. Only I would reverse-engineer it and add all the fat back in so it would taste amazing. I came home confident.

'What did my mother say?' asked Sami. I could tell he was nervous.

'That she trusted me completely and the entire dinner is in my hands.'

'Was she home?' he replied. 'Didn't she have her wisdom teeth removed this morning?'

The phone rang. It was my mother-in-law. I gave Sami a dirty look.

'Make sure you practise your butter chicken before Eid,' she said. 'Walmart is the only store that sells boneless, skinless halal chicken thighs. Your recipe won't work with any other cut of meat. Remember, Ramadan ends in two weeks.'

'That was your mom. Just thanking me for taking over,' I told Sami.

'The Novocaine might still be in her system. Where are you going?'

'Walmart. I have to buy my groceries.'

I threw the three forbidden ingredients the low-fat ladies said to omit from the recipe into my grocery cart: cashew butter, regular butter and whipping cream. I bought a package of boneless, skinless chicken thighs from the large section of halal meat to make my first sample of butter chicken. Back at home, I marinated the chicken overnight, fired up the barbecue the next day, grilled it, chopped it into bite-size pieces and then cooked it in its fat-bath. As Zayn took the first bite, I felt as if I were a contestant on *Hell's Kitchen*.

'It's yummy,' he said as he chewed. I looked triumphantly at Sami.

'I didn't even taste it,' I told him, 'because I cooked it during the day while I was fasting. And it still tastes amazing.' Zayn put his fork down after three bites.

'What's wrong?' I asked, a little worried. 'Why aren't you finishing it?'

'I'm too full.' As the fat congealed on his plate, I realized what had happened. The curry was too rich.

'It's not too late to decorate the house,' Sami said. 'There's no shame in it.'

'Yes there is,' replied Maysa. 'Remember the year she hung dented milk jugs from the ceiling?'

'Are you talking about the bloated sea creatures?' said Sami.

'They were whales!' I explained.

'Because that makes much more sense,' replied Maysa.

In defence of the whales, the girls were young and I felt we had to compete with Christmas, the grandaddy of all religious holidays. Muslims don't have holiday icons like Santa Claus or Frosty the Snowman, because we have a hysterical fear of worshipping things other than God and our holidays centre around themes like starvation and near-child sacrifice. Abraham's almost-sacrifice of his son is much harder to celebrate with papier mâché than you might think, so I improvised. I took two-litre plastic milk jugs and transformed them into giant blowfish, or whales, depending on the angle and time of day, and suspended them from the ceiling. I thought it was inventive.

'What have whales got to do with Eid?' asked Maysa.

'The milk jugs have a natural whale-like shape, so I just went with it,' I replied.

'Moon and stars would have been more appropriate than giant mammals hanging in our living room,' said Sami. 'At least there are two suras in the Qur'an named after the stars and the moon.'

For some reason, we don't fear worshipping the cosmos, so celestial themes are all the rage in Muslim decorative paraphernalia. The moon comes from the aforementioned calculation of dates, and the stars were used at one time to aid in navigation. It's not very mystical, but it's what we've got to work with. I just hadn't thought of them in time. But I felt a bit defensive in light of my inedible curry.

'So what? There are suras named Cow and Fig,' I replied. 'Should I make a papier mâché cow jumping over a Fig Newton?'

'See, you don't take the holidays seriously,' replied Sami.

'Or your religion,' said Maysa.

'Yeah, well, I take my chicken seriously. I'll add less fat next time around and it should be fine.'

The next day, I stocked up with fresh chicken to try again. I asked Sami to clean the barbecue – I'd gummed up the grill with chicken pieces.

'Zarqa!' I went outside and saw that the barbecue had been left on all night.

'How did that happen?' I asked.

'You didn't turn it off,' he replied. The chunks of chicken stuck to the grill were now grey ash.

'So the gas was on all night. There must be an automatic mechanism to stop it,' I said anxiously.

'The house could have blown up. That would have stopped it.'

'How come the grill racks don't sit evenly like before?' I asked, ignoring his sarcasm.

The outside of the barbecue now bowed out slightly and the racks were at a precarious angle.

'I guess the extreme heat caused the barbecue to bend,' said Sami as he stared at his luxury, top-of-the-line natural-gas bar-becue with the sadness of a man who had just lost his dog. 'It's not too late to hire a caterer.'

'You don't think I can do this?'

'A woman's place is not in the kitchen, it's in the board-room.'

'Are you saying I'm sexist for wanting to cook?'

'I'm saying your skills lie elsewhere,' said Sami. He was right. But a part of my psyche was pulling me in another direction. All my life I had been obsessed with my career, but not today. Maybe it was all my female ancestors who had grilled, roasted, fried and baked various animals into tasty dinners for their families that were calling out to me. My kids had never been as excited about my professional accomplishments as they were now that I was planning a meal. Zayn had asked to invite his friends and teachers from school. And, rallied by his enthusiasm, I'd asked my sister-in-law Samira to post the open house on her Facebook page. Nearly a hundred people had RSVP'd. The train had left the station. So the chicken was inedible and the barbecue was barely functioning. That didn't mean anything. Sami could tell I was determined, and wisely stopped talking to me.

As the final days of Ramadan slipped by, my mother-in-law got really worried.

'Did you go to Walmart to buy the rest of the meat? You'll need at least thirty packs for the number of people you've invited.'

Thirty packs? I did some mental arithmetic – she was right. I should have been stockpiling for weeks. What if I had to debone two hundred chicken thighs in one night? I'd never deboned a single chicken thigh before. But then I thought of the large halal butcher section at Walmart and relaxed. Everything would be fine.

'Just five days before Eid,' said Sami, trying not to make eye contact.

'I know,' I said breezily as I put my coat on and headed to Walmart, picturing how remorseful Sami would be for doubting me yet again.

I returned the greeter's hello with incredible enthusiasm and grabbed myself a trolley. There was no way I could carry thirty packets at once. On my way to the coolers I picked up some elegant napkins and paper plates. I had this under control. I parked my cart.

And stared down at the completely empty halal section. A

wave of panic rushed over me. Just the other day, it had been full. Why hadn't I stocked up then? In a panic, I searched for help. I saw a man with a badge that said MEAT MANAGER. His name tag said RALPH.

'Excuse me, Ralph? Hi. There was a lot of meat in that section yesterday,' I pointed to the empty shelf. 'What happened to it?'

Ralph regarded me for a few moments. 'I think people bought it.'

'But Eid is in, like, five days.' I could feel my heart attempting to leave my chest.

'What's Eid?' asked Ralph.

'It's a celebration at the end of Ramadan, where Muslims don't eat or drink anything for thirty days.'

'Shouldn't you be dead?' asked Ralph.

'Of course we eat food, but only after sunset,' I answered as patiently as I could. I think I was screaming. 'But we celebrate the end of the month by eating. A lot. In fact, we eat so much food that day it probably makes up for the whole month.'

'That's ironic,' said Ralph. 'Kind of defeats the purpose of fasting.'

'I really, really need the meat. I have a lot of cooking to do.' I lowered my voice and leaned in towards him conspiratorially. 'And I haven't even started.' The effect on him was less dramatic than I'd hoped.

'Well, that wasn't very smart. You should really plan ahead next time. But I'll check in the back.' He came back a few moments later.

'Nope, all out.'

'But Eid is our biggest holiday. You're the only place that sells this type of meat!' I said.

'Really? I'll make sure we're properly supplied next time,' said Ralph. 'When is Eid next year?'

I dialled my mother-in-law from the parking lot in a panic. I had ruined Eid.

She didn't badger me. She was practical. I had over a hundred people coming to my house in just a few days and I had no meat. She sent me to a halal butcher that had just opened. She'd heard a rumour that they carried boneless, skinless chicken thighs. And yes, that's what counts as a rumour in our community.

I started the car with a heavy heart. I usually avoid halal butcher shops. They carry – and prominently display – tongues, feet and brains, pieces of meat that scare me. If I were trying to make a Frankenstein version of a cow, a halal butcher would be my one-stop shopping destination.

The butcher's door chimed as I opened it. Nearly every halal shop resembles an eccentric pawnshop; there's meat, of course, but there are also other unusual items that regular butchers' shops don't carry, like clothes, bangles, prayer mats and tea sets. This one was no exception. I could have redecorated my living room with the trinkets on offer. The place was stuffed to the gills, and everyone wanted something that wasn't meat. I desperately needed to talk to the owner, but he was behind the cash register, talking with a man who had spotted a gilded framed photograph of the Kaaba, which was conveniently on sale.

'That's a nice picture,' said the man.

'It's an alarm clock,' said the owner. The man leaned in with interest. Let me explain. In a Muslim country, there is someone giving the azan, the melodic call to prayer, from the top of a mosque five times a day. If you don't want to hear the morning azan, which can be very early, too bad. But Muslims who live in a non-Muslim country have special alarm clocks that play the azan in a tinny, pre-recorded voice to announce the beginning of each prayer. And the alarm clocks are disguised as pictures of the Kaaba and the surrounding structures. We would never choose an alarm clock in the shape of a cow because Muslims have that horrible fear of accidently worshipping something with a soul. Plus we have bad taste – Muslim decorative paraphernalia is always some sort of calligraphy on black velvet, kind of like all the artwork involving Elvis. I do not have an alarm clock in my house because I value silence. I just pray when it's time to pray. When I visit my parents, I force them to turn off their alarm clock because I'm worried I'll have a heart attack when it goes off in the middle of the night.

'How does it work?' asked the man in front of me. Oh no, please, God, save me, I thought as the owner took it down from the shelf.

The man and the owner spent the next twenty minutes wrestling with the clock's byzantine buttons. Each clock has to be programmed, since the times for the five prayers change with the location of the sun, as well as with the latitude and longitude of the owner. I tried hard to be patient, but I was starting to get a headache from the lurching sounds of the azan as dials turned this way and that. Fasting is supposed to teach you patience, but it wasn't really working. So to calm myself down I stared at the sparkly shalwar kameez on display. A hot-pink tunic and trousers set caught my eye. Now that I thought about it, I had nothing to wear on Eid. Eventually the prayer clock proved it could provide service in any hemisphere, the man left and my turn came up.

'Nice choice,' said the owner as he put my outfit in a bag. 'Pink works well with your skin tone.' Only in a halal shop will you get fashion advice from the butcher.

'Thank you,' I replied, adding a few bangles to my purchase. 'I feel I'm forgetting something though.'

'Sometimes people come here for meat.'

Meat! Yes! This man was a genius.

'Do you carry boneless, skinless chicken thighs?' I asked confidently, hoping that my voice alone could conjure up these rare pieces of meat.

'What do you need them for?' he asked.

'To fill potholes,' I quipped.

The owner just stared at me. I felt that Ralph would have appreciated my sense of humour.

'I'm making butter chicken for Eid,' I told him. 'I'm having an open house.'

'We only carry the boneless, skinless thighs in a forty-kilo box.'

'That's perfect. That exactly how much meat I need.' I didn't know if it was, but it sounded like a lot, which was more than I currently had.

'You sure? It's normally a restaurant special order. How many people are coming?'

'Over a hundred. It's for the whole community. I've asked everyone I've met to come over, even people I don't know very well.' The owner continued to stare at me. I realized he must wonder why he didn't count as somebody I hardly knew.

'Would you like to come?' I asked. 'Here's my address.' I scrawled it on a piece of paper.

After getting directions to my house, the owner sold me the box of meat for the wholesale restaurant price of $220. It was an Eid miracle.

I came home and showed Sami the hot-pink shalwar kameez.

'What do you think?' I asked.

'Is it edible?' asked Sami. I ignored him and put out the meat to defrost.

The next morning, I set to work. I tossed the garlic, ginger and onions into the blender. Inspired, I set aside the mortar and pestle, and instead pulsed the spices in my coffee grinder. Like a miracle, they were perfectly crushed. I was going to be fine.

I marinated my meat in a mixture of yogurt, cumin, coriander, black pepper, lemon pepper, paprika, garlic and ginger.

The next day, I took out the marinated pieces, started the barbecue and balanced the meat on the wobbly grill.

Once the meat had cooled, I chopped it into bite-size pieces and then made the curry, mixing the spices, onions, ginger and garlic and then adding the meat. Now for the delicious fat – a little less than my first attempt – and a few teaspoons of sugar. My stomach was growling like crazy. This was going to be great.

'Can you make curried chickpeas too?' asked Zayn. They were his favourite. I couldn't say no.

I opened five cans of chickpeas and emptied them into another pot while cooking the butter chicken. The key to curried chickpeas is to add gravy from the chicken to make it taste richer, and then to throw in a little fresh tamarind. Technically, you're supposed to push the thick brown substance through a sieve to separate the sour, thick juices from the pulp, but I was in too much of a rush so I threw in chunks of tamarind instead.

'There are brown lumps rising up in your chickpeas,' said Maysa.

'I can take those out,' I said, and scooped them up with my strainer.

I grew cocky with my success with the chicken and chickpeas; I tried to make curried meatballs the next day. Maysa helped me shape the meatballs and I cooked them, but in my haste I had overspiced the ground beef and the meatballs were too salty and pungent with spices.

'My throat burns,' said Maysa.

My mother-in-law, the wise sage, had me add potatoes and boiled eggs to the meatball pot to absorb the extra salt and spices. The dish was tolerable if you didn't sop up too much of the gravy. I surveyed my new mountain of food. Sami stood beside me and for the first time looked impressed.

'Good job,' he said.

'And you doubted me,' I replied smugly.

'Mama, can I invite the guy who's pruning our tree?' asked Zayn.

'Of course you can. See, our kids will always remember this,' I told Sami. 'A mother who can cook for her entire community.'

'He says he's vegetarian,' said Zayn, coming back in. I looked at my meat-based and meat-infected food. Zayn looked at me expectantly.

'I'll cook a vegetarian dish,' I told Zayn.

'You don't have to do this,' said Sami.

'Yes, she does,' said Zayn. 'I fasted a whole month and I deserve a party.'

'Plus, it's tradition,' I said.

'Not really,' replied Sami, and went out to make sure the local soccer stadium was ready for the Eid prayers. It was the largest open space in the city. I waited till he left and then phoned my mother-in-law.

'Make French-cut green bean curry,' she said. 'It's easy.'

French-cut green beans come frozen in plastic bags. I

bought ten. As I cooked them in spices, the phone rang. It was my friend Ruby.

'There's a sale on chafing-dishes at the local Co-op,' she said. 'You need to buy at least five.'

'Why do I need those?' I asked.

'You have too much food to just put out,' she said. 'It'll keep getting cold and you can't keep warming stuff up in the microwave.'

She was right. We planned a trip together to pick up the food warmers. When I hung up the phone, I realized I had lost track of time. The green beans on the stove had transformed from a bright green bundle into a swampy brown mess.

'That's not an appetizing colour,' said Maysa as she inspected the food. I called my mother-in-law immediately.

'Chop up red bell peppers and add them to the green beans,' she said. 'It'll make them brighter. And put in a cup of pine nuts.'

I did as I was told and the vegetables perked up. The tree pruner had his food. I could relax. Eid was in two days but I felt like I had it under control.

In the evening, Sami came home.

'Where's all the food?' he asked, looking at the huge mess in the kitchen.

'In the garden,' I replied. It was September and we were having a cold snap, so the back yard worked perfectly as cold storage, since there wasn't enough room in the fridge for all the food.

'Don't worry, animals don't like curry,' I told Sami.

'That's not what I'm worried about,' he replied. 'But now that you mention it, that could be a problem too.'

Faeeza came over to retrieve a cooking pot she had loaned me.

'Do you remember that one year when you left all the food for your dinner party outside?' she asked.

'Sure, it was winter,' I said. 'Everything stayed cold.'

'We had a few days where it got warmer.'

'Oh yeah.'

'Your food melted and refroze several times,' she said.

'You still served that food?' asked Sami incredulously.

'No one died,' I replied.

'That's your litmus test for a good dinner party?' asked Sami.

'I only ate what I brought,' said Faeeza. I assured both of them that, according to the weather forecast, there weren't any warm days or nights coming up.

'Saudi Arabia just declared Eid for tomorrow,' said Sami, checking his email.

'What?' I yelled. 'Ramadan is supposed to be thirty days!'

I should have known better.

Ramadan can last either twenty-nine or thirty days, depending on when the new moon is sighted to signal the end of the month and the beginning of a new one. We aren't content with having a shifting date; we also argue ferociously about how to determine what constitutes a new moon. There are two sides to the debate: those who calculate the birth of the new moon using relative angles of the horizon, and those who argue that we must use the naked eye, as the Prophet would have done. But then the argument gets mired in where the moon is being sighted. Is the moon sighted locally (how you define 'locally' is another debate) or do we go with the first sighting globally? And which council of Muslims determines the validity of the sighting? Both methods are religiously valid, and since we don't have a pope or central authority, each year we rehash the familiar arguments. And each year there's confusion about when to begin Ramadan and when to end it. So sometimes you'll have two or three Eids in one community, depending on how divisive things get.

Most Muslims agree that the problem, as usual, is Saudi Arabia. The Saudis declare Eid regardless of calculation. They're kind of like the Americans when it comes to the moon: they believe everyone should just follow them. This year, they'd screwed me up. I phoned my friend Zabiba.

'I will do this only for you and no one else,' she said. I brought over my extra ground beef, onions and coriander – enough for a hundred samosas.

Ruby agreed to pick up the chafing-dishes for me. Faeeza took a few things home to her fridge to keep them safe. Sami and the kids went on a cleaning marathon. I had planned to use the next day to sort out the house but we had just lost twenty-four hours. Zayn had to call his friends who didn't know Eid was tomorrow, because Muslims hadn't known either until a few hours before.

After the morning Eid prayers, our family rushed home to set up the food. I filled the chafing-dishes with boiling water and lit two small cans of chafing fuel under each. I watched the stream of people come through the door, Muslim and non-Muslim alike. Even my children's teachers came. Mr Lloyd, Maysa's physics teacher, arrived with his family. He sat with a group of Muslim men and asked an innocent question.

'So why do Muslims insist on dating the new moon by eye, when we can calculate the day in advance?' He inadvertently started a violent conversation. I made a mental note to give white people topics to avoid on Eid. We mixed up the men and women and Muslims and non-Muslims. No one seemed to mind.

In my Eid panic, I had forgotten to make dessert, but people brought lots of sweet things as hostess gifts. I had also forgotten about tea and coffee, but Faeeza and Ruby, veterans of my botched dinner parties, boiled water in a large pot and went next door for the cream and sugar. Maysa ran the dishwasher a couple of times since we were using real cutlery and dishes. (I had accidentally abandoned the disposable ones in my rush out of Walmart.) The kids were busy serving friends and family. Against all odds, they were able to hang out with all the people who mattered in their lives – and some who didn't.

As I watched people eat food that I had cooked and not choke and throw it in my face, I felt a sense of pride. Our house was packed to the gills with people who didn't have enough space to sit, because I had forgotten to get extra chairs, but they sat on the staircase all the way up, and in the bedrooms. It was a sort of controlled chaos. I had created a brand-new tradition. My mother-in-law came up to me.

'You did well,' she said. 'I know it wasn't easy.'

'Thank you for all your help,' I replied, grateful beyond words. 'I couldn't have done it without you. You're the only one who had faith in me.'

'Of course I did. It was self-serving. I am now officially retiring from Eid dinners because you can do it.'

I could do it. Sort of. I basked in my semi-chaotic glory.

After the endless parade of people finally left our home around 1 a.m., I lay on the couch while Sami rubbed my aching legs, which were sadly still hairy.

'You did it,' he said a little incredulously.

'And you doubted me.'

'Yep,' he said. 'But you have a way of being resourceful.'

'Your mom was a huge help.'

I looked at the pile of hostess gifts in the corner. Sami opened one. It was a prayer alarm clock.

'Hey, a very nice man from the halal butcher store gave that to us,' said Sami. 'He said you were staring at it a lot in his shop.'

'Only in hatred,' I said as I got up and quickly pulled a large cardboard box from the storage cupboard. I put the alarm clock in it. I'd donate the box to a local charity. I was sure there was an eccentric non-Muslim farmer out there who'd always wanted to be awakened before sunrise to the Arabic chant of prayer.

'I want to do this again for next Eid. One day, in the future, my children will tell their grandchildren, "Our mom cooked Eid dinner from scratch without any casualties."'

'Except for the barbecue,' said Sami nostalgically.

'Sorry about that,' I said. 'We'll get it fixed. But I promise to be totally prepared in the future. When is Eid next year?'

'Google it,' replied Sami.

Dying, Muslim-Style

I learned about death from a mouse.

One January I was cleaning out the storage room in the basement when I saw tiny droppings. In the freezing cold Saskatchewan winter, a mouse had found refuge in our basement and survived on a forgotten bag of chocolate coins.

'That was dumb,' I chastised myself for forgetting about the candy tucked in amongst the Eid supplies.

The mouse had to go. I figured if I cut off its supply of chocolate, it would move on to more fruitful pastures somewhere else. It worked. The droppings disappeared. But a few days later, I noticed droppings in the kitchen. With four kids leaving their own food droppings, the mouse had hit pay-dirt. Its biggest problem was whether it would die of diabetes or a heart attack.

Disgusting, I thought as I swept away the mess. Sabreena told me to get glue traps. They were effective, the only caveat being the mouse would still be alive, though stuck fast. I was fine with that – I could handle a mouse – but I was anxious to get it out of our home. I had read about all the diseases a mouse carries and, cute as it was, it had to go. And anyway, there was no way I'd catch it before Sami got home from his shift that night.

As I watched TV in the living room after the kids had gone to bed, I heard a muffled squeaking sound coming from the kitchen. It couldn't be. As I slowly opened the cupboard door, I could make out a mouse shape on the glue pad just before I screamed and ran back to the couch. I called Sami at work.

'What's wrong?' he asked, concerned. 'You're out of breath.'

'Can you do me a favour when you come home from work later?'

'I'll be pretty late, but sure. Do we need some milk?'

'No, there's a mouse caught in a trap in the cupboard,' I said. 'I want you to kill it.'

I am a terrible assassin, outsourcing the dirty work to others.

The next morning at breakfast, I asked Sami how he had killed the mouse.

'I just took the trap, put it in a plastic bag and threw it in the garbage can outside,' he said. 'It was minus forty, so the mouse wouldn't have lived long.'

As the horror of what he said seeped in, I felt a little dizzy. I sank slowly into a chair, speechless. This was my first experience with death and I had botched it completely. My mouse had had a horrible death and I was to blame. I hadn't seen my mouse through till the end. It had died alone and afraid and very, very cold, all because I had wimped out. 'But you could have killed it first,' I said, trying to keep the trembling out of my voice.

'I was tired,' said Sami. 'It was 2 a.m. and I wasn't in the mood to look for a two-by-four to smack a mouse on the head.'

I was pretty sure that mouse murder wasn't an actual crime, so there was no point in calling 911. And why was I blaming poor Sami when I had set the whole thing in motion in the first place? I learned a valuable lesson that day: death is scary and final and needs to be treated with respect.

As the memory of the mouse slowly started to fade, it was replaced by an increasingly morbid fascination with death rituals for humans. A few months later, I attended a funeral with Sami and my South African friends Faeeza and Ruby. We sat hushed in the Victoria Avenue Funeral Home's pew-like seats. It almost felt like a church as I closed my eyes and listened to Dr Faiz Mansoor's son give a short talk about his father. This was the first Muslim eulogy I'd ever heard. We pop our dead bodies into the ground before they even have a chance to get cold, so we don't get much time to put pen to paper. But Dr Mansoor's son had managed to write a few words, and they were lovely.

I turned to Faeeza. 'Can I give your eulogy when you die?'

'I'm not dying and being buried here in Regina,' she replied quickly.

'That's the perfect opening sentence: "Faeeza Moolla said she would never die in Regina, Saskatchewan, and yet here we are today ..."' I needed to write that down quickly before I forgot. God only knew I wouldn't get enough time after she was dead. I pulled out a pen from my purse and scrawled my sentiment on the back of a Safeway receipt.

The old Muslim rulebook has pretty firm dictates on death: you die in Vegas, you get buried in Vegas (although you may want to leave a note explaining what you were doing in Vegas to your conservative Muslim relatives). And if someone you love dies, you'd better move quickly – Muslims do not wait for far-flung relatives to show up before holding a loved one's funeral. That one sticks a bit for me. I understand the need to bury as soon as possible, but sometimes I think this practice is taken too literally.

I turned to Sami.

'When I die, do you promise to be at my funeral?'

'Why wouldn't I be?'

'What if you're far away and don't make it back in time?'

Sami held my hand. 'If anyone would miss a funeral it would be you. I'll die and you'll be in Timbuktu shooting a movie or something.'

'I'd come back,' I said. I wouldn't leave you, cold and abandoned like some poor mouse, I thought, but kept that to myself since it was still a sore point between us.

'OK, no more speaking,' said Sami and we left the pews for the funeral prayer in the larger room.

The simple pine coffin sat in front of the congregation. We lined up in rows as if for a normal prayer at the mosque but the *janaza*, the funeral prayer, was performed without any bowing. As we gave our condolences to the family and started to leave, I stared curiously at the closed coffin. Sometimes I wondered if open-casket funerals, like some religions hold, gave mourners a stronger connection to the deceased.

'If we popped this open for a sec, do you think the family would mind?' I asked as Sami steered me quickly past the body, out of the funeral home and into the car.

When we were safely back at home, Sami sat me down. 'OK, what is it with you and death all of a sudden?'

'Muslim funerals are too simple,' I said. 'If we speak about the dead, it would help give us closure. Bring more dignity to the death.'

'Muslims can have eulogies if they want,' said Sami. 'But I like our simple funerals.'

Muslims have a very basic three-part ritual: wash the dead, pray for the dead, bury the dead.

'Other religions have open caskets, singing and speeches and fancy printed programmes. It's basically a gala,' I said. 'Is it my fault if they've made their funerals so enjoyable?'

'I don't think that's what they were going for,' said Sami. 'And besides, religion is not always supposed to be about having fun.'

Islam couldn't be accused of that, I thought.

'I joined the DBWC at the mosque,' I announced the next day at dinner. 'Faeeza said they were looking for volunteers.'

'What's a DBWC?' asked Inaya.

'A dead-body-washing committee,' I said.

'They have a committee for washing dead bodies?'

'Yep. That way, there's no running around finding volunteers at the last second. But they were having trouble finding volunteers because people were squeamish about washing the dead. So I signed up.'

Muslim bodies have to be washed immediately after death, so there isn't a lot of time to talk people out of their reticence. It's important to have a standby group of volunteers; the Muslim community in Regina was growing and many elderly parents who had joined their children in Canada were passing away.

'Why would you want to wash dead bodies?' grimaced Maysa.

Good question. Weirdness aside, it was a good thing to volunteer in the community. But a tiny part of me felt that service in the DBWC would redeem me for not giving my mouse a good death. A few weeks later I got a call from Faeeza.

'Jameela's mother just passed away.'

Neither of us knew Jameela very well. Faeeza, Ruby and I entered the solemn Victoria Avenue Funeral Home. Jameela sat weeping, surrounded by friends who were consoling her. She was too distraught to speak so we quietly gave our salaams and entered the embalming room. Aunty Nadia was waiting for us. She was in charge of the committee.

'There are some rules we should review before we begin. Everything you see today will be kept in the strictest confidence. No talking about anything to anyone ever. In fact, no talking at all. Understood?'

I didn't know why she kept staring at me. But she was right: if you happened to die with a tattoo on your behind that read I LOVE AHMED, and Ahmed was not your husband, you were safe with the DBWC.

Jameela's mother's body was lying on the table, covered by a white sheet with just her face exposed. All my desire to view a dead body suddenly disappeared and I found myself frozen to the spot. Faeeza prompted me to move forward, and I willed my feet to take the few steps to reach the body. Because we don't believe in embalming or making the deceased look more presentable with make-up, Muslims see the dead exactly as they looked when they passed away. Jameela's mother had died of a heart attack and she was wearing a plain cotton shalwar kameez. She looked serene, but there was no colour in her face.

'Put on your latex gloves,' said Aunty Nadia as she took a pair of scissors and cut the clothes off the deceased. To preserve her dignity, none of us was allowed to look at her naked body. We would wash the body with camphor-scented water while it lay underneath the sheet.

Aunty Nadia plugged the corpse's ears and nostrils with cotton balls and then gently pushed on her stomach to expel anything that remained. Then she washed the body's private parts, which continued to be covered by a piece of cloth. The hair was washed next, followed by *wudu*, which is a washing ritual Muslims perform before prayers. Lastly, we performed the ghusl, a general washing that starts with the right side of the body and then takes care of the left.

The hardest part was lifting the body to wash her back. Four of us heaved her on to her side as Aunty Nadia washed.

'Now we know where the term "dead weight" comes from,' I said as I tried not to lose my grip on the wet body.

Aunty Nadia looked at me as she finished washing the back of the body.

'Jokes will not be tolerated at this time,' she said.

'I wasn't joking, I was just commenting on how heavy the body is,' I replied, a little scared.

'We don't comment about the body,' said Aunty Nadia. 'Ever.'

After the body was washed and dried, we wrapped it in three pieces of plain white cotton.

We gently lifted Jameela's mother into a simple pine coffin. Traditionally Muslims don't use coffins, so that the body returns quickly to the earth, but since most cemeteries require a container by law, we pick the simplest one possible, which is usually a pine box.

When we were done, Jameela's family came in to see their mother for the last time. I took off my latex gloves and sat in the waiting room. Aunty Nadia sat down beside me.

'Perhaps the DBWC isn't the best way for you to help out,' she said.

'What?' I said. 'But why?'

'Because you said inappropriate things during a very solemn occasion.'

'I just say what I'm thinking.'

'And that's exactly the kind of person we don't need,' said Aunty Nadia. 'I think you should join the Social Committee instead. It suits your personality.'

I went home desolate.

'You got kicked off the DBWC?' said Sami. 'That's a first.'

'Aunty Nadia was very intimidating,' I replied. 'And not a lot of fun.'

'Like I said before, you really need to take the "fun" out of "funeral".'

'I don't want Aunty Nadia in charge of my body when I'm dead. Will you wash me when the time comes?'

'No, I think I'll be too busy grieving to do that,' said Sami. 'I imagine Aunty Nadia will be able to get along fine though.'

'But she'll be no-nonsense and dictatorial and won't let anyone crack a few jokes or question God's alleged view on things.'

'Sounds like the kind of woman I like,' said Sami.

I looked at him.

'To wash a dead body,' he finished.

A year later, Inaya came home one Saturday afternoon from visiting with her grandfather.

'Dadu's looking a little yellow,' she said.

Sami's father seemed fine, a little tired, but he was seventy-seven and still working full-time as an ear, nose, throat and allergy specialist. He went to the doctor that Monday and found out why he was turning yellow: there was an obstruction in his bile duct. It was biopsied and found to be cancerous. A CT scan revealed Stage IV cancer, which was inoperable. In the space of a few days he went from a happy, if tired, grandfather of eleven grandkids to a man with six to eight months left to live. He shut down his practice the following week and started a steep decline in health. The year before, Sabreena and Munir, Sami's sister and brother, had moved back to Regina, and we were grateful that we could be together.

Just before he learned about his illness, my father-in-law had planned to take all of his grandkids for umrah, the lesser hajj. With his youngest grandchild, Medyna, turning seven, he wanted to show them the religious sites himself. The plane tickets and hotels were all booked and paid for. The evening he told us about his illness, we knew the trip would be cancelled. He cried more about not being able to take his grandkids on the pilgrimage than about getting cancer. It was the only thing he wanted to do before he died, he told us.

'Should we still go?' I asked.

'No,' said my mother-in-law, wiping her eyes with a Kleenex. 'We all need to be together now.'

We made the decision to keep him at home for palliative care instead of taking him to the hospital. Each of his grandkids took turns spending time with him. The older ones read from the Qur'an, particularly sura Yaseen, traditionally read to the dying for comfort. The younger ones talked to him, massaged his legs and rubbed his fingers, which he enjoyed. Eventually he was too weak to walk and needed to use a wheelchair. Sami, Munir and Amir, Sabreena's husband, were strong enough to carry him, and took turns taking him to the washroom to bathe him. My mother-in-law never left his side, always reading his favourite prayers to him.

When it became difficult for him to eat, Sabreena would try and coax him to drink a liquid meal replacement to keep his strength up, but he protested that it would elevate his blood sugar. It was the only thing he had control over any more and no one had the heart to tell him that it didn't matter. He had always been very health-conscious.

My mother-in-law asked us to keep to our normal routines, so I began cooking the food for our open house on Eid, the end of Ramadan. It was now tradition. The community looked forward to my chaotic dinners and I never disappointed. Samira had put out the invitation on Facebook.

But on Thursday, two days before Eid, my father-in-law was no longer able to eat. He stopped being able to communicate so his children had to guess what he needed. We quietly cancelled our Eid plans. On Friday, to keep him hydrated, my mother-in-law gave him a sponge dipped in Zam Zam water to suck. That evening, on the last day of Ramadan, four months into his illness, we gathered in his bedroom to exchange presents. Our family has a tradition where we put everyone's name in a bowl and each person pulls out a name – kind of like a secret Santa, if Santa were brown, Muslim and lived in Mecca instead of the North Pole. You buy the person whose name you've drawn a present and we keep the price to $20. My father-in-law loved watching the great Eid gift exchange, and so we all exchanged our gifts on the floor of his room, kneeling beside his bed and hoping he could at least hear the laughter of his family.

'Really?' said Maysa, looking at the e-reader cover I had bought her. She had requested that it be hand-decorated and I had taken two colourful postcards with a cow and a giraffe, cut them to fit the front and back of the cover and attached them with rubber bands.

All of us bantered back and forth about our gifts while my father-in-law lay in his bed, looking like he wanted to speak but clearly unable to.

That night while my mother-in-law slept fitfully beside

him, Munir, who was sitting vigil on a chair near the bed, noticed his father nod slightly and then stop breathing. Muhammad Anwarul Haque died peacefully in his bed at 3 a.m. on 18 August 2012, the thirtieth day of Ramadan.

Sami, Munir and Amir washed their father's body along with other male members of the community that afternoon. They tried to arrange the funeral and burial for that evening, but it was Saturday and the cemetery needed twenty-four hours' notice to prepare the plot, which delayed the funeral by a day – thankfully giving time for relatives, including my parents, to arrive.

The next day was Eid and his janaza was conducted after the Eid prayers. Almost five thousand people prayed for my father-in-law that day in Evraz Place, a large events complex. Afterwards, we drove in a long caravan of cars to the cemetery.

It quickly became clear that our imam was worried that certain male community members didn't want women to take part in the funeral. My father-in-law was a deeply religious man and would never have accepted this double standard; the imam was told that all the women in the family would be participating completely in the burial and that anyone who objected wasn't welcome. My father-in-law would have approved. In some respects he had been traditional and in other, more surprising, ways he hadn't. He had enrolled his wife in two universities – McGill in Montreal and the University of Manitoba – when he married her in Bangladesh, because he didn't know which province he'd settle in and he didn't want her to miss out on her education.

As we stood watching my father-in-law's simple coffin being lowered into the ground, I pictured him as he was when he was healthy: looking after his beloved plants in his greenhouse and teaching his grandkids how to nurture flowers and vegetables in Saskatchewan's very short growing season. I remembered the blueberry plant he had just bought from the nursery. Because he was too sick, he had asked me to look after it. I had, of course, killed it instantly, then panicked and planted an impostor in its place. I had the kids bring him the blueberries.

I wonder if he knew, I thought to myself as his pine box reached the floor of the grave. Sami lowered himself into the hole, opened the box and gently rolled his father on to his side so he faced Mecca. Anwar had wanted to make sure he was facing north-east in his grave and had asked his eldest son to perform this final task. Munir helped pull his brother out.

I looked around the cemetery, at the other Muslim head-stones in the same row. When my father-in-law moved to Regina, he had purchased plots for himself, his wife and their three kids. It occurred to me, standing there with my two fellow in-laws, Samira and Amir, that there were no plots for the three of us. In fairness to my father-in-law, he probably hadn't been thinking about future spouses. I stared covetously at the four remaining spots.

'It should be first come, first bury,' I told Samira. I knew I was out of line, but I was bursting with so many tumultuous emotions, one of them needed to come out.

'I don't think we should discuss this right now,' she said, trying to move away from me. I remembered Aunty Nadia's reprimand and behaved myself for the rest of the funeral.

The next day I asked the family if I could write an obituary for the Regina *Leader-Post*. I wanted a chance to capture and celebrate this man I had come to know and love so well. I wrote about how the Islamic Association of Saskatchewan had been created at the home of my in-laws. Back then, the community consisted of a handful of Muslim families, and he and my mother-in-law used to host potlucks in their home until a tiny mosque was purchased. It was a room above a hair-dressing salon and had been affectionately referred to as 'the Mosque above Murphy's'. The family contributed their edits and the obituary made the paper.

A few days after it was published, a freelance reporter for the *Globe and Mail* called. The reporter felt that my father-in-law had been a pioneer in the Regina Muslim community and wanted to write a longer piece about him. She interviewed Sabreena, and two weeks later there it was. The obituary was the longest one I had ever read in the paper and took up nearly an entire page. As I spread it out on the breakfast table that morning, I thought it was better than the eulogy we hadn't had a chance to give him.

A few days later, as Sami and I lay in bed, 'How are you feeling?' I asked.

'Sad, but you know, he lived a full life, lived long enough to see all his kids get married, some to nuttier partners than others . . . And he got to know all his grandchildren as well.'

Maysa, now eighteen, was the oldest grandchild, and he had lived long enough to know that she was about to leave for McMaster University.

'I'm glad our kids were able to grow up with their grand-father and to help take care of him,' I said.

Emigration to a new land and untimely death had separated us from the chance to know our own grandparents. We lay there quietly for a bit.

My father-in-law's death had been so sudden. I hadn't even believed it when he told me he was sick. But he had been loved and cherished by his entire family. I hoped for the same experience when my time came. Death teaches us to value life, and now I had two losses that had taught me to value the people we love and never take them for granted: my father-in-law, who loved his family above all, and a tiny mouse who loved chocolate.

'I forgive you for the mouse,' I said to a surprised Sami as I hugged him tight.

Acknowledgements

I would like to thank Tina Horwitz, my television agent at Vanguarde Artists Management, for introducing me to Samantha Haywood, my book agent at Transatlantic Literary Agency. She in turn introduced me to Kate Cassaday, my editor at HarperCollins. If it weren't for the incessant nagging of these three women, I would never have finished this book. And I'd like to thank Lennie Goodings, my editor at Little, Brown in the UK, for shepherding the international version of the book. I would also like to thank my kids, Maysa, Inaya, Rashad and Zayn, for their constant refrain of 'Aren't you done yet?' I hope I didn't humiliate the four of you too much with the poo and pee stories. When you guys grow up, you can write your own memoirs to straighten the record. Your grandparents are depending on it.

Finally, I'd like to thank my Muslim community, who live in constant terror of being represented on TV or in a book or whatever my next project is. I couldn't have done it without you. You complete me.